"A book for all Mafia lovers. During my six years as an under-cover FBI agent in the mob, I had many a laugh at the humor of gangsters. A must read."

Joe Pistone, a.k.a. Donnie Brasco

THE OFFICIAL BOOK OF

Mob Humor

Malcolm Kushner

Foreword by Henry Hill

Robert D. Reed Publishers ▪ Bandon, OR

Robert D. Reed Publishers
P.O. Box 1992
Bandon, OR 97411
Phone: 541-347-9882; Fax: -9883
E-mail: 4bobreed@msn.com
Website: www.rdrpublishers.com

SOFT COVER EDITION:
Editor: Cleone Reed
Cover Designer: Cleone Reed
Book Designer: Debby Gwaltney
Cover Image: Mafia Gang © Gerald Senger, istockphoto.com
Cartoon illustrator: Kenny Durkin

ISBN 13: 978-1- 934759-51-6
ISBN 10: 1- 934759- 51-1

Library of Congress Control Number: 2011935423

Manufactured, Typeset, and Printed in the United States of America

Dedication

For Chris Griger and Sam Kushner—my "family"

Friends of Ours

T his book wouldn't exist without the help and encouragement of many people. First and foremost was publisher Bob Reed who had the idea for the book and asked me to write it. Dr. Christine Griger provided her usual invaluable editing skills. And Deborah Decuir graciously offered her insights on numerous drafts of the material.

If a picture is worth a thousand words, then a picture of praise goes to Cleone Reed for the cover design. Compliments for typesetting and layout go to Debby Gwaltney. And the artist behind the sparkling cartoons is Kenny Durkin. Grateful appreciation also to Sam R. Kushner who captured the "real me" for the author photograph.

Many thanks also to Henry Hill, Frank Cullotta, Louis Ferrante, Joe Pistone and Mayor Oscar Goodman for their kind words about the book. They are five stand-up guys!

Kudos also to Lisa Schinelli Caserta, Matty Goldberg, Heather Tamarkin, Amy Tamarkin Taylor, Phil Taylor, Amanda Borrelli, Justin Herzfeld, Elizabeth Woodge Stover, and Larry Weinsteen—they know why. Or maybe they don't.

Table of Contents

Foreword

If you've ever seen the movie *Goodfellas*, then you already know I used to be a mobster. The movie was based on my life. Actor Ray Liotta played me. And you'll also know that humor was important to me and my colleagues. We told a lot of jokes and had a lot of laughs. In fact, *Goodfellas* reflected this so accurately that some people think it was a comedy rather than a mob movie.

Of course, mob humor can be a little darker than the regular kind. Like in the movie when Joe Pesci shoots a flunky in the leg because he didn't bring a drink fast enough. Later when the flunky complains, Joe Pesci shoots him again. When it's pointed out that the guy is dead, Pesci says "I'm a good shot. Whaddaya want from me?" Like I said, mobster humor can be kind of dark.

And a lot of these mob guys take themselves very seriously, so you have to throw in a little bit of humor. I always used it to get along. You have to see the humor in things just to preserve your sanity. For example, I think it's funny that I took a plea deal and went into witness protection to avoid going to prison. Yet now I live in a gated community—and a patrol car comes by every 45 minutes.

By the way, my time in witness protection was the basis for another movie – *My Blue Heaven* starring Steve Martin. It's not reality-based like *Goodfellas* but it was inspired by all the problems I had adapting to life in the slow lane in the middle of nowhere. It's pretty funny. It's even listed in this book in the chapter on mob comedies.

Oh yeah, I'm supposed to talk about this book. One of the most famous lines in *Goodfellas* comes when I tell Joe Pesci's character that I think he's funny. Pesci replies: "Funny how? I mean, funny like I'm a clown? I amuse you? I make you laugh?" I thought of that line when I was reading *The Official Book of Mob Humor*. Because this book is funny. It's amusing. And it made me laugh. It will make you laugh too.

—Henry Hill, Former Lucchese crime family associate
immortalized in the movie *Goodfellas*
You can learn more about Henry Hill at
http://www.goodfellahenry.com/

Introduction

Investigators looking into the collapse of a building in New Jersey have made a major discovery. The collapse was caused by weak concrete purchased from the mob. They sold contractors diluted cement—too much sand and gravel, not enough whacked bodies. Ba-da-boom. Or should I say Ba-da-bing?

Humor and the mob have a long history together. Wise guys have always been as well known for cracking jokes as cracking heads. Of course, ordinary, law-abiding citizens might not think their jokes are funny. But that's all right. They have ways of making you laugh!

In this book, I've gathered a wide assortment of humor related to organized crime around the world—from the Yakuza and Triads in Asia to the Russian and Italian Mafia in Europe to the American mob in the United States. The type of humor is also varied. It ranges from quips, quotes and jokes to cartoons to real headlines and news stories. Want to know where I got this stuff? I ain't talking. It fell off the back of the truck. And if you subpoena me, I'll take the Fifth.

One thing I will say is this. Contrary to popular stereotype, organized crime in the U.S. has never been the exclusive domain of Italian-Americans. Since the Roaring Twenties, Jewish gangsters and Irish racketeers have been just as prominent as Mafia crime lords. And today, they're joined by the Mexican Mafia, Russian Mafia and criminals from many other ethnic groups. America has always been a melting pot. And criminal activity is no exception.

Here's the point. Cement has no skin color. If someone puts you in concrete boots and pushes you off a pier, you're still going to be dead no matter who pushed you. You know what I'm saying?

So sit back. Relax. And discover the wit, wisdom and foibles of the mob. C'mon, I'm going to take you for a ride.

— Malcolm Kushner
Menasha, Wisconsin   April 2011

CHAPTER ONE
Wise-Guy Wisdom

Two mob soldiers, Frank and Bobby, were walking through the woods after dumping a body. Frank saw an old lamp on the ground. When he picked it up, a genie appeared. The genie said, "As a reward for freeing me, you can have one gift: infinite money, infinite wisdom or infinite beauty." Well, everyone always called Frank dumb so he chose infinite wisdom. The genie said, "Done," and disappeared in a cloud of smoke. Frank just stood there frozen with his head surrounded by a halo of light. Finally, Bobby whispered, "Say something." Frank sighed and said, "I should have taken the money."

It's an old joke, but it says a lot about mobsters. Some of them are dumb. Some of them are smart. And it's always about the money.

While many people associate muscle with the mob, it's actually brains that play a more important role in advancement. Sure you've got to be tough. But any knuckle-dragger can slam a baseball bat across a union official's knees or pistol-whip a shopkeeper who won't pay for protection. If that's all you've got, you'll stay in the lower echelons of the organization. The ones that rise to the top— Al Capone, Meyer Lansky, Lucky Luciano, Mickey Cohen, Carlo Gambino, to name a few—all had brains. You can't be a dummy and run a multimillion dollar criminal enterprise.

Many observers have remarked that being at the top of an organized crime family isn't that different from being the CEO of a large corporation. Of course, corporate CEOs aren't usually retired in a hail of bullets. Maybe that makes the wisdom of these mob bosses even more valuable. They pay a much higher penalty for failure.

In this chapter, you'll hear what mob leaders have to say about a wide variety of topics—in their own words. Advice includes everything from dealing with bankers and bosses to paying taxes, carrying guns and buying elections. You'll also hear from some of the lower-level people. Why? Because the school of hard knocks—especially when you're giving them—is a great teacher. So even the thugs and muscle men have some knowledge you might find useful. Hey, that's why they're called wise guys.

John Gotti: A View from the Top

John Gotti became boss of the New York-based Gambino crime family in the mid-1980s. He was known as the "Dapper Don" because of his expensive suits and the "Teflon Don" because of his ability to beat indictments in federal court. It has been estimated that the Gambino family made over half a billion dollars from illegal activities while Gotti was in charge. He was finally sentenced to prison where he died of cancer in 2002. *People* magazine described his legacy as "the most feared and celebrated gangster since Al Capone." Here are some thoughts from the man some have called the last, great godfather.

"He who is deaf, blind and silent, lives a thousand years in peace."
– John Gotti

"I know where my mistakes are, where I made my mistakes. They're too late to remedy, you know what I mean?"
– John Gotti

"FBI stands for 'Forever Bothering Italians.'"
– John Gotti

"Always be nice to bankers. Always be nice to pension fund managers. Always be nice to the media. In that order."
– John Gotti

" Don't carry a gun. It's nice to have them close by, but don't carry them. You might get arrested."
– John Gotti

" If you think your boss is stupid, remember: you wouldn't have a job if he was any smarter."
– John Gotti

"If he had an Italian last name, they would've electrocuted him [on Bill Clinton]."
– John Gotti

"I'm in the Gotti family; my wife's the boss (after being asked whether he was the boss of the Gambino crime family)."
– John Gotti

Un-friend him.

Miscellaneous Mob Wisdom

"Always overpay your taxes. That way you'll get a refund."
– Meyer Lansky

"You can get a lot more done with a kind word and a gun, than with a kind word alone."
– Al Capone

"There's no such thing as good money or bad money. There's just money."
– Charlie "Lucky" Luciano

"Never open your mouth, unless you're in the dentist chair."
– Sammy "The Bull" Gravano

"One hand washes the other...both hands wash the face."
– Sam Giancana

"There's always free cheese in the mousetrap."
– Salvatore Avena

"There are three sides to every story. Mine, yours and the truth."
– Joe Massino

"Why take a chance on a candidate who might lose? You can always buy them after the election."
– Santo Trafficante

"When I sell liquor, it's called bootlegging; when my patrons serve it on Lake Shore Drive, it's called hospitality."
– Al Capone

Mob Wisdom from the Movies

On February 22, 2008, the *New York Post* reported that Francesco Fiordilini while sentenced for killing a drug dealer apologized to the court and Italians for being a negative stereotype. And he blamed the entertainment industry for making him a real-life mobster caricature. "Although I made all my drastic decisions on my own, Hollywood intensified my love for that life and in the process blindsided what being Italian meant," the Bonanno crime-family associate explained.

Hey, stop him before he watches another mob movie!

But maybe he has a point. After all, you can learn a lot from cinematic explorations of the mobster lifestyle. Here are a few insights from some of them.

Be Cool
Darryl: What do you tell a man with two black eyes?
Nothing; he's already been told twice.

A Bronx Tale
Calogero 'C' Anello: It was great to be Catholic and go to confession. You could start over every week.

Bullets Over Broadway
Rita: For me, love is very deep, but sex only has to go a few inches.

Get Shorty
Harry Zimm: I once asked this literary agent, uh, what kind of writing paid the best... He said, "Ransom notes."

Lock, Stock and Two Smoking Barrels
Barry the Baptist: When you dance with the devil, you wait for the song to stop.

Mad Dog and Glory
Women, you can't live with them and you can't kill them!
– Frank Milo

Mad Dog Time
Ben London: You can never really know the size of a person's brain until you have to clean it off the carpet, and let me tell you, Sleepy Joe had quite a brain.

The Mexican
Frank: Guns don't kill people—postal workers do.

Mobsters and Mormons
Carmine "The Beans" Pasquale: Leave the gun. Take the granola.

Robin And The Seven Hoods
Little John: When your opponent's sittin' there holding all aces, there's only one thing left to do: Kick over the table.

Snatch
Bullet Tooth Tony: You should never underestimate the predictability of stupidity.

Triggermen
Andy Jarrett: Love is blind; friendship closes its eyes.

The Whole Nine Yards
Jimmy "The Tulip" Tudeski: It's not important how many people I've killed. What's important is how I get along with the people who are still alive.

Favorite Mob Proverbs

Blood is thicker than water—especially on the floor.

Nothing is certain but death and taxes, and we don't pay taxes.

Actions speak louder than words—especially if you're gagged.

Strike while the iron is hot or use a baseball bat.

There is more than one way to skin a cat or anything else.

Every family has a skeleton in the closet; some have it under the basement floor.

The last straw breaks the camel's back, but a crowbar works good too.

Don't cut off a nose to spite a face—cut off the ears.

It's better to be pissed off than to be pissed on!

Everything I Need to Know
I Learned from the Mob

1. There's no problem that cannot be overcome by violence.

2. The more you run over a dead body, the flatter it gets.

3. There's no such thing as too much hair gel.

4. Anything can fall off the back of a truck.

5. Never torch the wrong storefront.

6. Wearing a wire clashes with every shirt color.

7. You always look better than your mug shot.

8. Friends may come and go, but enemies accumulate.

9. Anything worth fighting for is worth fighting dirty for.

10. Being indicted makes you lose your memory.

11. If you think there's good in everybody, you haven't met everybody.

12. When in doubt, say "Fuggedaboudit."

CHAPTER TWO
Headline Hits

Newspapers around the world take great delight in finding puns to use in the headlines of stories about mob activities. The practice is most common in New York City where rival dailies the *New York Post* and the *Daily News* pounce on every opportunity available. For example, a witness at a racketeering trial testified that mob boss Vincent "Vinny Gorgeous" Basciano was so worried someone might wear a wire to rat on him that he made his underlings strip before meeting with him. On June 28, 2007, this news was trumpeted by headlines in both the *New York Post* and the *Daily News*. Or as they put it, "Illegal Briefs – Mobster Made His Capos Strip" (*New York Post*) and "It's a rattrap! Mob guy had clothes call, trial told" (*Daily News*).

Why haven't the mobsters taken out these headline hit men? Who knows? Maybe the pen really is mightier than the sword.

In this chapter, you'll find examples of headline humor as executed by various newspaper editors. But maybe I shouldn't say executed. I don't want to give anyone any ideas.

Separate checks?

Mobster Sleeps with the Swishes

(*New York Post*, May 1, 2003)

"A Mafia turncoat told a stunned courtroom yesterday how he gunned down his mob boss—because he was gay."

Remade Men; Gotti Ordered Do-Over Mob Inductions

(*New York Post*, November 19, 2004)

"A New Jersey-based Mafia family flunked out of mob school.

"The late Gambino boss John Gotti ordered the DeCavalcante family to repeat their inductions of 'made' members because they failed to follow the rules during the original ceremonies—and considered them invalid."

Judge Gives Wise Guy a Weigh Out of Jail!

(*Daily News*, New York, March 5, 2007)

"Judge Blockhead is at it again.

"A controversial jurist whose mouth keeps getting him into trouble granted an early release to a Mafia enforcer last week after noting the wise guy lost weight in prison and didn't look so scary anymore, the *Daily News* has learned."

'Eraser' Head of the Mob Persico Retried for Rival 'Rub Out'

(*New York Post*, November 7, 2007)

"Mafia kingpin Alphonse 'Allie Boy' Persico wanted to 'erase' a rival to his Colombo crime-family throne when he orchestrated the man's 1999 murder, prosecutors charged yesterday."

'Pizza' Fugitive Is 'Duh!'Livered

(*New York Post*, November 5, 2007)

"A 20-year fugitive wanted in the notorious Pizza Connection drug-ring case was ready for his close-up when he stepped off a plane at JFK Airport—but all he got was a mug shot, The Post has learned.

"Enrico 'Kiko' Frigerio—unaware that he was still under federal indictment—was arrested by FBI agents as he returned to New York while assisting a Swiss TV crew filming a documentary about his colorful life, sources say."

'Mob Baker Killed Man for Dough'

(*New York Post*, November 14, 2007)

"A Queens pizza man and a Brooklyn baker didn't want to pay the piper—so they arranged to have him whacked instead, prosecutors charged yesterday in Brooklyn Supreme Court.

"Carmine Polito, 49, a compulsive gambler and the owner of an Astoria pizzeria, and Mario Fortunato, 60, the owner of Greenpoint's Fortunato Bros. bakery, allegedly plotted the murder of a Genovese loan shark and his cousin during a friendly card game, so that Polito wouldn't have to cough up $60,000 he'd borrowed."

I'm Don For...

(*The Mirror*, December 18, 2008)

"MAFIA Godfather Gaetano Lo Presti, 52, was found hanged by a belt in his cell yesterday hours after being held in a raid in Sicily."

Gangsters Push the Envelope

(*The Courier Mail*, February 21, 2002)

"Japanese post offices have been giving special treatment to mail sent by and to gangsters, the government-run Postal Services Agency said yesterday.

"A recent survey conducted by the agency revealed that 344 out of 1312 post offices throughout the nation have exchanged gangsters' mail in special bags between post offices so that it would be delivered promptly."

Meat-Shop Mob Guy Will Never Loin

(*Daily News*, New York, November 8, 2008)

"Call these Bonanno gangsters a bunch of beef jerkies for getting caught on a government bug planted in a Staten Island meat market.

"The feds are breaking the gangsters' chops over incriminating conversations picked up on the listening device that targeted recently deceased Bonanno soldier Joseph (Junior) Chilli, who was a fixture in Belfiore Meats on Victory Blvd. along with the sausage, chopped meat and steaks.

"'He [Chilli] sat in a chair right next to the Lotto machine in the front,' a source told the Daily News. 'The place was like his headquarters.'"

'Concrete' Evidence-Stoolie Paid Mob for Cement Biz

(*New York Post*, February 12, 2008)

"It's called 'How to Succeed in Business Without Getting Whacked by the Mob.'

"Joseph Vollaro, the mobbed-up Staten Island trucking exec threatening to bring down the Gambino crime family by squealing, has laid out for the feds in damning detail how he paid and paid, and then paid some more, to do business with the Mafia."

Mobster a Violet Man, Hairstylist Testifies

(*New York Post*, March 5, 2009)

"A purple-headed hit man joined the colorful cast of characters at a mob murder trial in Brooklyn yesterday.

"Hairstylist Frank Selvaggio said he became friends with Charles Carneglia in the early 1990s and would visit his home twice a month to cut his hair, but the reputed wise guy changed his coif's color on his own on 'numerous' occasions—sometimes with startling results.

"Once, Selvaggio was stunned to see Carneglia, 62, walking down the street in Ozone Park with purple hair."

Barber Misses Jail by A Hair in Mafia Case!

(*Daily News*, New York, July 24th 2007)

"It was a close shave yesterday for an East Harlem barber who nearly went to prison for lying to the FBI about his Mafia clientele.

"Instead, a federal judge sentenced Claudio Caponigro to a year's probation for playing dumb when FBI agents asked him to identify photos of some of his mobster pals."

Yule Be Sorry—Rat Squeals on Gotti Over $50 Xmas Gift

(*New York Post*, December 2, 2004)

Crack'eteering—Mobster Jokes Way Through Guilty Plea

(*New York Post*, December 24, 2002)

"Wise-cracking wise guy Anthony 'T.G.' Graziano yesterday acted more like the life of the party than a man expecting to spend the rest of his life in prison as he prepared to plead guilty to racketeering conspiracy charges.

"The 62-year-old reputed Bonanno consigliere was more gagster than gangster during his court appearance, as he fired off a flurry of jokes with the ease of a seasoned stand-up comic."

He's in Fitness Protection; Ex-Mobster's a Hit Coaching Little Leaguers

(*New York Post*, July 15, 2001)

"Former mob figure Michael Franzese ordered up a hit this weekend.

"But Franzese's soldiers were happy 11-and 12-year-olds looking to take a few good whacks—on the ball field.

"Once a shrewd Colombo crime family captain, Franzese has gone from goodfella to good sport as a highly respected Little League coach in the upscale San Fernando Valley community of Encino."

Sicilian Mafia
De–Capo–Tated

(Daily News, New York, April 12, 2006)

"THE LEGENDARY Mafia super-boss known as 'The Tractor' ran out of gas yesterday as Italian cops capped a four-decade manhunt with an anti-climactic raid on his Sicilian hideout.

"Bernardo Provenzano, 73, was captured when authorities tailed a bundle of clean laundry sent by his wife to a sheep farm near Corleone—the town that inspired the fictional mob family's name in 'The Godfather.'"

Is Mob Big Shot Helping Son Learn Big Words, Or Is It a Sagacious Plot?

(Daily News, New York, May 2, 2008)

"Flippant. Sagacious. Thespian.

"Vocabulary-building words for a 7-year-old or coded messages to the Mafia?

"The FBI has been analyzing the contents of letters Bonanno crime boss Vincent (Vinny Gorgeous) Basciano writes to his young son, which include college-level words he wants the mob scion to look up in a dictionary.

"Because Basciano is caged under conditions usually reserved for terrorists—he's suspected of plotting to kill a judge and prosecutor—all communications with the outside world are scrutinized."

Chips Off the Old Cell Block; Sons Follow in Footsteps of 2 Imprisoned Crime Bosses

(*New York Times*, June 17, 2000)

"Many men who run huge enterprises and reach the summit of their professions want their sons to follow in their footsteps. But on this Father's Day, two sons who tried to follow their fathers' career paths have instead followed them into prison.

"In both cases, it was a family business. The fathers are John J. Gotti, the convicted boss of the Gambino crime family, and Carmine J. Persico, the imprisoned leader of the Colombo family."

Mob 'Killer' Just Whack–Y

(*New York Post*, February 11, 2009)

"A top Gambino hit man with a reputation for being a bit batty was so comfortable with killing that he even offered his services to the FBI, an agent testified yesterday.

"'Is there anybody you want me to whack?' Charles Carneglia, 62, allegedly asked Special Agent Robert Vandette, who had stopped by the mobster's Brooklyn junkyard to ask questions in 1995."

Mobster Didn't Kill Time, Just His Boss

(*Daily News*, New York, November 25, 2004)

"EXTORTION? No-show jobs? No problem. But ask a wanna-be wise guy to do a hard day's work and it could cost you your life.

"That was the lesson jurors learned yesterday from a top Gambino crime family turncoat who told them about the 1997 murder of construction foreman who was killed because he worked a gangster too hard."

Mobster's Set to Get Slice of Prison Life

(*Daily News*, New York, October 13th 1998)

"It's the end of an era.

"Luchese mobster Ralph (Raffie) Cuomo, who founded the original Ray's Pizza in 1959 and still manages the place, is going to prison for using the Prince St. pizzeria to sell heroin along with slices."

A Great Duh–Fense.
Caracappa Lawyer Awol;
Mistrial Bid Is Shot Down

(*Daily News*, New York, April 1, 2006)

"THE DEFENSE IN THE MAFIA cops trial suffered a meltdown yesterday after a federal judge ruled that eleventh-hour revelations by a jailed Mafia underboss were not cause for a mistrial. Brooklyn Federal Judge Jack Weinstein also rejected one motion to dismiss for lack of evidence.

"But what really irked the veteran jurist was lawyer Edward Hayes skipping town without permission on a critical day for the defense."

Tats All, Folks—Tattoos Could Convict
'Sammy Bull' Hit Man

(*New York Post*, October 7, 2003)

"An assignment to crush mob canary Salvatore 'Sammy Bull' Gravano was no skin off this reputed wise guy's back, the feds say.

"Dozens of tattoos that coat Thomas 'Huck' Carbonaro's frightening physique read like a mob hit man's bible—and could be used as evidence against him if federal prosecutors get their way."

26

The First Bada–Bank
Feds Charge Gambinos in Mo. Takeover
(*Daily News*, New York, July 29th 2004)

"EVEN TONY SOPRANO never thought of this one.

"The Gambino crime family actually took over a bank as a cover to run a nationwide Internet porn rip-off, the feds have charged."

Gotti Brats Go Legit;
Trio Bids To Be Capo-Talists
(*New York Post*, August 21, 2005)

"It's a new 'family business' for the Mafia-to-meatballs Gotti crew. Victoria Gotti's three pampered pretty boys, Carmine, John and Frankie Agnello—grandsons of the late 'Dapper Don' John Gotti—are finally getting jobs, opening a chain of restaurants called 'Ciao Bella' in honor of their mom and also a tanning salon."

Yakuza Given a Helping Hand
by 'Mr. Fingers'

(*The Observer*, January 3, 1999)

"Only one person dares give the finger to Tokyo's gangsters—the Japanese Mafia's favorite Yorkshireman.

"Wearing a polka-dot tie and white surgeon's coat, he looks the model of a sober scientist. In the antiseptic corridors of Bradford's St. Luke's Hospital, they call him 'The Prof'.

"But Professor Alan Roberts is well connected to a more sinister world. In Japan's notoriously violent Mafia, gangsters who owe him a debt of honor call him 'Mr. Fingers'.

"Roberts, Britain's leading skin scientist, is exporting false hands to Tokyo in a multi-million-pound deal which is providing a boost for the National Health Service. His biggest customers are Yakuza—members of Japan's underworld. They hack off their own fingers as part of a strict code of honor, to pledge loyalty to their bosses and atone for wrongs. Surgery to disguise the stigma is unreliable. Most opt for false limbs to conceal their life of crime."

'Goldie' Finger—Unlikely Mobster Rats on
Massino in 'Hit' Parade

(*New York Post*, July 14, 2004)

"The 'blond sheep' of the Bonanno family—a gangster with the unlikely name Duane 'Goldie' Leisenheimer—took his place in mob history yesterday as the eighth turncoat to finger from the witness stand reputed godfather Joseph Massino for a slew of mob hits."

'License' to Die in Mob Hit

(*New York Post*, April 29, 2003)

"[Joseph Garofano] screwed new license plates on his car to protect his identity—but the plates belonged to the wife of Anthony Capo, the DeCavalcante soldier driving the killer's car, prosecutor Miriam Rocah said."

Casting-Call Mobster Wanted Wrong Kind of 'Break'

(*Boston Globe*, June 16, 1999)

"Talk about bad actors.

"An event for wannabe Mafia actors at an East Village eatery turned into a real-life shakedown when a thug allegedly threatened to break the owner's leg for not paying protection money."

Mob Figure May Have Been Butt of Joke

(*Boston Globe*, June 16, 1999)

"There were three major developments yesterday in the continuing saga of the wise guy and the FBI bug that may or may not be stuck in his nether regions."

CHAPTER THREE
Murder and Mayhem

Aman walks into a church confession booth and says, "I have sinned."

The priest asks, "What did you do?"

The man says, "I committed a murder."

The priest says, "Take a drink out of the holy cup and you will be forgiven."

Another man walks into the confession booth and says, "I have sinned."

The priest asks, "What did you do?"

The man says, "I hijacked six trucks."

The priest says, "Take a drink out of the holy cup and you will be forgiven."

A third man walks into the confession booth and says, "I have sinned."

The priest asks, "What did you do?"

The man says, "I peed in the holy cup."

The first two men could be mobsters but not the third. Why? Because there are certain things even a mobster won't do.

In the convoluted world of mobster codes and conduct, there are rules that must be followed. You never squeal to the authorities. You never disrespect the boss. You never wear a wire. You always obey orders. Yet despite fealty to their code of honor, mobsters commit many acts that would never be considered proper by anyone else. Killing. Drug running. Loan sharking. Money laundering. Gambling. Prostitution. Hijacking. And a myriad of other sordid activities. At least they're always nice to their mothers!

In this chapter, you'll find some quotes, stories and other items relating to the always illegal and often violent activities of the mob.

The Mob on Murder

"I never killed a guy who didn't deserve it."
– Mickey Cohen

"Goodfellas don't sue goodfellas. Goodfellas kill goodfellas."
– Salvatore Profaci

"A little violence never hurt anyone."
– Benjamin Ruggiero

"You can imagine my embarrassment when I killed the wrong guy."
– Joe Valachi

"I don't know who shot me. It was somebody that didn't like me, I guess."
– Dutch Schultz

"You never get no back talk from no corpse."
– Frank Capone

A Good Deed

A guy who had just died arrived at the pearly gates. St. Peter looked through his book to see if the guy could enter heaven. He looked through the book several times and furrowed his brow. "This is very perplexing," said St. Peter. "You never did anything really bad in your life. But you never did anything really good either. If you could point to just one really good deed, I could let you in."

The guy thought for a minute. Then he said, "Well, there was this one time I was driving down through the city and saw a bunch of mobsters assaulting someone. I slowed down to see what was going on and they were just beating the crap out of this poor little shopkeeper. Infuriated, I got out of my car, grabbed a tire iron out of my trunk, and walked up to a big goon who was punching and kicking the shopkeeper. As I walked up to him his pals formed a circle around me. So I smashed the big goon over the head with the tire iron. Then I yelled at the rest of them, "Leave this poor, innocent shopkeeper alone! You're all a bunch of psychopaths."

Impressed, St. Peter asked, "When did this happen?"

The guy said, "Oh, about three minutes ago."

Mobsters in Heaven

Three New York mobsters are killed in a shootout with a rival crime family. They arrive at the Pearly Gates and see St. Peter.

"Dis is where we belong," says the mob leader.

"I'm sorry," replies St. Peter, "but I don't see any of your names on the admittance list."

"Look up our records," says the mobster.

"I have," said St. Peter. "You've robbed, you've maimed and you've killed. There's no way God would allow you into heaven."

"Fuggedaboudit," says the mobster. "I knows God would let us in if you ask Him."

"If you insist," replies St. Peter. "Just stay put and I'll be right back." With that St. Peter knocks on God's door and enters.

"Excuse me, Lord," says St. Peter, "but I've got three mobsters waiting outside the Pearly Gates looking to get into Heaven. They insist they belong in Heaven. They don't, but I told them I would ask you."

"Judge no man by his outward self," God responds. "Bring them to me and I will decide."

St. Peter goes back to get them. A few minutes later, he hurries back to God and says, "They're gone."

God asks, "The mobsters?"

St. Peter says, "Yes, and the Pearly Gates."

Headline Hits: Murder and Mayhem

Grave Consequences
No Body's Home in Mobster Grave!
(*Daily News*, New York, September 17, 2006)

"If the feds ever find gangster William (Wild Bill) Cutolo's corpse, there's a tombstone and empty grave waiting for him at the Cemetery of the Resurrection in Staten Island.

"Carved in black stone under a likeness of Cutolo and his wife, Peggy, are the words: 'Cherished Husband, Dad and Poppy. Our Love Is Forever and Always. Until We Meet Again. We Love You Beyond The Moon.'

"'His picture is there, but he's not there,' said Cutolo's sister, Barbara DePalo, 67. 'I just find talking to him there peaceful.'"

Bury Clever Mobsters—
Two-Deck Coffins Hide Dead
(*New York Post*, October 7, 2003)

"A mobster undertaker in the real-life Sopranos crime family used 'double-decker coffins' so that whacked victims could be buried secretly in the same box as legitimate clients of his funeral parlor, a Manhattan jury was told.

"Turncoat mob capo Anthony Rotondo told stunned jurors that one of the oldest members of New Jersey's DeCavalcante family, Carlo Corsentino—who lived to be more than 100—came up with the idea of using 'double-decker' coffins at his funeral home in Elizabeth, N.J."

'Plot' Thickens—
Judge Refuses to Exhume Mobster
(*New York Post*, June 10, 2004)

"A federal judge shot down reputed Bonanno boss Joseph Massino's bid to dig up a murdered capo's decades-old corpse yesterday after receiving a letter from the widow asking to protect her family from further heartbreak."

Judge Doesn't Dig Wise Guy
(*Daily News*, New York, June 10, 2004)

"Rest in peace, Sonny Black.

"A federal judge rejected yesterday a motion by lawyers for Bonanno boss Joseph Massino to exhume murder victim Dominick (Sonny Black) Napolitano."

Feds' Big Dig Hasn't Run Its Corpse
Investigators Seeking Buried Victims of
Mob Rub-Outs
(*Daily News*, New York, October 10, 2004)

"FBI agents have been digging for a week at a vacant lot on the Queens-Brooklyn border on the word of the latest tipster, who said Favara, and other mob victims, lay under the weeds."

The 'Hole' Truth – 'Undertaker' Dug Graves Upstate, Mobster Testifies

(*New York Post*, May 7, 2003)

"When DeCavalcante wise guys needed to dispose of a body quickly, they called 'The Undertaker'—a mobster buddy with a wealth of experience in digging graves, a Manhattan jury heard yesterday.

"Philip LaMella, a DeCavalcante soldier, earned his nickname by 'digging holes' for the mob at a property he owned in upstate Newburgh, former family capo Anthony Rotondo said yesterday."

What a Way to Get the Boot! Corpse Found at Long Island Mob Dig

(*Daily News*, New York, October 6, 2008)

"He died with his boots on—whoever he was.

"The search of a suspected Long Island mob burial ground that began last week turned up human remains Monday—a corpse wrapped in a tarpaulin, authorities said.

"Searchers said the corpse, unearthed at 3 p.m., was in a tarp cocoon—the traditional way mob hit men dispose of their kills—with shoe-clad feet sticking out."

The Phone Call

The phone rings and the maid answers.

Maid: Hello?

Mobster: Put my wife on the phone.

Maid: Just a minute.

Maid comes back after a minute: I'm sorry but she's indisposed in the bathroom.

Mobster: I said put her on the phone. Now!

Maid: She can't come to the phone right now.

Mobster: If you don't get her on the phone in two seconds I'm gonna come over there and pull your jaw from your face.

Maid: You don't understand; she's in there with another man.

Mobster: What!?!

Maid: Yeah.

Mobster: Listen, this is what I want you to do. I want you to shoot them both dead and then get rid of the gun.

Maid: I can't do that; I can't shoot anybody.

Mobster: You do it Now!

Maid: I can't!

Mobster: If you don't do it right now I'm gonna kill you and your whole family. Go do it now! I wanna hear the shots.

Maid: OK.

The mobster hears two loud shots over the phone.

Maid: I did it.

Mobster: Good. Whad'ya you do with the gun?

Maid: I threw it in the pool.

Mobster: Pool? What pool? We don't have a pool!? ... Is this 555-2264?

Speaking Truth to Power

Vinnie was one of the most feared mobster's in the city. That's because in his youth, he had angered one of the local crime-lords. As punishment, the crime-lord had both of Vinnie's ears cut off. He became mean and feared because of this mutilation.

Vinnie rose through the ranks of the mob and eventually became Godfather. The next day, Vinnie decided to flex his mob muscles a bit. He called in his chief enforcer, Guido. Vinnie said, "Guido, you've been very loyal to me. Tell me my friend, what is the first thing you notice about me?"

Guido replied, "That's easy, boss. You've got no f#%king ears."

Vinnie was furious that someone would blatantly insult him like this. He screamed at Guido, "GET OUT! YOU'RE DEAD!!"

Guido fled from his boss's office in terror.

Vinnie next called for Luigi. After telling him he now had a contract on Guido, he asked him the same question. "Luigi, you have been very loyal to me," said Vinnie. "Tell me my friend, what is the first thing you notice about me?"

Luigi also replied, "Well, boss, you've got no f#%king ears."

Vinnie, furious, screamed at Luigi, "GET OUT! YOU ARE DEAD! YOU ARE F#%KING DEAD!!!" He then called for Mario, his third capo.

On his way into the office Luigi stops him and says, "Listen Mario, the boss is in a mood. Whatever you do, don't mention anything about his ears." Mario thought it was a good idea and went in to see Vinnie.

Vinnie now told Mario that he had two contracts to fill. He then said, "Mario, you've been very loyal to me. Tell me my friend, what is the first thing you notice about me?"

Mario, heeding Luigi's advice, said, "I notice you are wearing contact lenses."

Vinnie was astounded. Vinnie said, "You must have really good eyes. How did you notice that?"

"Well, they had to be contact lenses," said Mario. "How can you wear glasses with no f#%king ears?"

Thoughts on Prison

"I don't like jail; they got the wrong kind of bars in there."
– Charles Bukowski

"If it weren't for my lawyer, I'd still be in prison. It went a lot faster with two people digging."
– Joe Martin

"A cement mixer collided with a prison van on the Kingston Pass. Motorists are asked to be on the lookout for 16 hardened criminals."
– Ronnie Corbett

"Don't do drugs because if you do drugs you'll go to prison, and drugs are really expensive in prison."
– John Hardwick

"The prison psychiatrist asked me if I thought sex was dirty. I told him only when it's done right."
– Woody Allen

"Homosexuality in Russia is a crime and the punishment is seven years in prison, locked up with the other men. There is a three-year waiting list."
– Yakov Smirnoff

The Factory

Mobster One: "I heard your factory burned down."

Mobster Two: "Shh. Not till next week."

The Kosher Nostra

Jewish gangster Abbe Caponovitch was dining at a restaurant in New York when members of the mob burst in and opened fire. Managing to stagger out of the restaurant, Abbe stumbled up the street to the block where his mother lived. As he clutched his bleeding stomach, Abbe crawled up the stairs and banged on the door of his mother's apartment, screaming, "Mama, Mama! Help me, Mama!"

His mother opened the door, eyed him up and down and said: "Bubbeleh, come in. First you eat; then you talk!"

Speaking of Jewish Gangster Mothers

Three Jewish mothers were sitting around and bragging about their children.

Freda says, "Benny graduated with honors from Harvard and now he makes $250,00 a year as a doctor."

Kitty says, "Sidney graduated with honors from Yale and now he makes $500,000 a year as a lawyer.

Ethel says, "Abe never did well in school, never went to college but now he makes $1,000,000 a year as a sports repairman."

The other two women ask, "So what's a sports repairman?"

Ethel replies, "He fixes hockey games, football games, baseball games."

You Know You're
An Over-the-Hill Mobster When...

You sink your teeth into a thick steak and they stay there.

Everything hurts, but you haven't been pistol-whipped.

You get winded playing cards.

Your idea of weight lifting is standing up.

You can't be tried by a jury of your peers because there are none.

Getting lucky means finding your car in a parking lot.

You look like your mug shot.

You don't need to say fuggedaboutit—because your friends can't remember anything either.

CHAPTER FOUR
It's Just Business

When Charles Anselmo, a mobster in the meatpacking industry, was asked whether any of his shipments contained horse meat, he replied, "Well some of it moos, and some of it don't moo." His answer reflects an attitude that underlies most mob activities—it's just business. Yeah, you can take things personally. But the smart money is on the mobsters who don't. Like Joseph "Joe Batters" Accardo who famously said, "Let him go. He cheated me fair and square."

Of course business for the mob includes activities such as killing and knee-capping. But when your revenues are based on arson, drug running, loan sharking, prostitution, gambling, wire fraud and similar enterprises, well hey, it's just business.

And business is booming. (Not just because of all the guns going off!) As organized crime in some countries has come under attack by government officials, the mob in other parts of the world has grown and prospered. It wasn't that long ago that the word "Mafia" was associated mainly with criminals in Italy and the United States. Today it's more like a United Nations of crime. You've got the Russian Mafia. The Mexican Mafia. The Israeli Mafia. The Albanian Mafia. The Canadian Mafia. The Korean Mafia. And the list goes on. Throw in the Yakuza from Japan and the Triads from China and it's amazing the entire world hasn't been hijacked.

In this chapter you'll find humor about the various criminal operations that engage mobsters everywhere from America to Zaire. Infiltrating unions. Bribing elected officials. Silencing opponents. Disposing of bodies. Hey, it's just business.

The Trial

The mobster was on trial, facing a possible life sentence, but his lawyer bribed a juror to hold out for a lesser charge. After hours of deliberation, the jury returned a verdict carrying a maximum of ten years in prison.

Afterwards, the lawyer approached the juror. "You had me worried! When the jury was out so long, I was afraid you couldn't pull it off."

"I was worried too!" answered the juror. "The others all wanted to acquit him!"

The Student

"Dad, everybody at school makes fun of me. They say I'm the son of a mobster."

"OK, son. Don't worry. I'll go and talk to them."

"Dad, make it look like an accident."

The Watch

An old Mafia Don is dying and he calls his grandson to his bed. "You listen to me. I want you to take my chrome plated .38 Smith-and-Wesson so you will always remember me."

"But Grandpa, I really don't like guns. Howzabout you leave me your Rolex watch instead."

"Shuddup an listen. Some day you're gonna run da business, you're gonna have a beautiful wife, lotsa money, a big house and maybe a couple of kids. Some day you're gonna come home and maybe find your wife in bed with another man. Whadda you gonna do then... point to you watch and say, "Time's up?"

Retired Mobsters

Two old mobsters met while walking on the beach in Miami. After chatting awhile they discovered they'd both run criminal operations in New York and retired to Florida.

One said, "Yeah, I had a big warehouse. It was destroyed in a fire. I took the insurance money and moved here."

The other said, "Yeah, I had a big warehouse too. It was destroyed in a flood. I took the insurance money and moved here."

The first one said, "So? How do you start a flood?"

The Voice

A wise guy drives to Atlantic City, dumps a body in the ocean and walks along the beach back to his car.

Suddenly a deep voice says, "Dig!"

He looks around. Nobody's there. He thinks he's hallucinating.

Then he hears the voice again. "I said dig!"

So the wise guy starts digging in the sand with his bare hands and finds a small chest with a rusty lock.

The deep voice says, "Open!"

The wise guy takes his gun and bangs on the lock. When the chest opens, he sees a lot of gold coins.

The deep voice says, "Go to the casino."

The casino is nearby, so he takes the chest to the casino.

The deep voice says, "Roulette!"

So the wise guy changes all the gold into a huge pile of chips and goes to a roulette table.

The deep voice says, "27!"

The wise guy takes the whole pile and puts it all on 27.

The crowd can't believe it. They're absolutely silent as the croupier throws the ball.

It lands on 26.

The deep voice says, "Shit."

Good News/Bad News

A Mafia guy came home from work in a pretty good mood.

"How was work, Honey?" his wife asked.

"I got good news, and I got bad news," he told her.

"Well," pondered his wife, "I'll guess I'll take the good news first."

"OK, get this," he boasted. "The boss gave me an important new job, and he's paying me FIFTY GRAND! I start tomorrow."

"That's fantastic, Honey! Did you tell your best friend, Vinnie, yet?" she excitedly gushed.

"I said there was bad news, too, baby," he frowned. "Vinnie's dead."

"Oh my God, no! Vinnie was the best!" she cried. "He gave the kids a nice present every Christmas! When did he pass away?"

The Mafioso looked down and shook his head. "Tomorrow."

The Eulogy

A famous Jewish mobster dies, a man well-known as a crook, loan shark, drug dealer, and hit man.

The mobster's brother, himself a mobster, asks the local rabbi to do the service.

"I'll pay you ten thousand dollars if you say something nice about my brother."

The rabbi is a serious, religious man.

"I really can't do that. Your brother was a crook."

"Listen, rabbi. I'll give you a hundred thousand if you say something nice about my brother."

"I'm sorry. A rabbi can't lie."

"OK, here's my final deal. I'll give you a quarter of a million dollars to say something nice about my brother."

The rabbi thinks about all the repairs that need to be done to the temple roof and the new Sunday school that he's been dreaming about. He agrees to the offer.

On the day of the funeral, the rabbi steps up to the podium and says:

"This man was a crook, a liar, a thief and a terrible human being. But compared to his brother, he was a saint."

The Collector

The mob was looking for a new man to make weekly collections from all the private businesses that they were "protecting". Feeling the heat from the police force, they decide to use a deaf person for this job; if he were to get caught, he wouldn't be able to communicate to the police what he was doing.

Well, on his first week, the deaf collector picks up over $40,000. He gets greedy, decides to keep the money and stashes it in a safe place. The Mafia soon realizes that their collection is late, and sends some of their hoods after the deaf collector.

The hoods find the deaf collector and ask him where the money is. The deaf collector can't communicate with them, so the Mafia drags the guy to an interpreter.

The Mafia hood says to the interpreter, "Ask him where da money is." The interpreter signs, "Where's the money?"

The deaf collector replies, "I don't know what you're talking about."

The interpreter tells the hood, "He says he doesn't know what you're talking about."

The hood pulls out a .38 and places it in the ear of the deaf collector. "NOW ask him where the money is."

The interpreter signs, "Where is the money?"

The deaf collector replies, "The $40,000 is in a tree stump in Central Park."

The interpreter, smiling, says to the hood, "He says he still doesn't know what you're talking about and doesn't think you have the balls to pull the trigger."

Signs It Won't Be a Good Sit-Down

When you arrive everyone stops making jokes about Jimmy Hoffa.

No seat for you at the table.

Guy standing in corner with big shovel.

Phone book open to florists' page.

Car out in front has trunk open.

The Walk

A mob enforcer named Frankie is driving his partner in crime Joey through the remote New York countryside. After driving into the foothills for about an hour Frankie pulls the car over to the side of the road. He tells Joey there is something in the woods they have to go see. After walking a short while it begins to become dark outside and Joey says, "Hey Frankie. It's cold and dark and very spooky in these woods. I gotta be honest I'm a little scared!"

Then Frankie turns and says, "You think you're scared Joey? I have to walk back to the car all alone."

Business Is Booming

A man walks up to a hit man and asks, "How are you doing?"

The hit man says, "Not so good. Business is murder."

The next day the man walks up to the hit man and asks the same question.

The hit man says, "I'm doing great! I made a killing yesterday."

Mobster Stress Relief

Picture yourself near a stream in the woods.

Birds are softly chirping in the cool mountain air.

Nothing can bother you here.

No one knows this secret place.

You are in total seclusion from the world.

The soothing sound of a gentle waterfall fills the air with a cascade of serenity.

The water is crystal clear.

You can easily make out the face of the person whose head you're holding under the water.

Feel better?

Thoughts on the Mob

"It is no secret that organized crime in America takes in over forty billion dollars a year. This is quite a profitable sum, especially when one considers that the Mafia spends very little for office supplies."
– *Woody Allen*

"The Bank of New York is in trouble because they were laundering money from the Russian mob. They ran as much as ten billion dollars through a single account. And they still didn't qualify for free checking."
– *Bill Maher*

"The mayor of New York City suspects that the Fulton Fish Market, a longtime New York City landmark, is now being controlled by organized crime. There may be something to that. Today I went there for lunch and I ordered lobster, and they served it tied-up, face-down, in a pool of butter."
– *David Letterman*

"The IRS! They're like the Mafia; they can take anything they want!"
– *Jerry Seinfeld*

"If you're a young Mafia gangster out on your first date, I bet it's real embarrassing if someone tries to kill you."
– *Jack Handy*

"Ours is a government of checks and balances. The Mafia and crooked businessmen make out checks, and the politicians and other compromised officials improve their bank balances."
– *Steve Allen*

"Intellectuals are like the Mafia; they only kill their own."
– *Woody Allen*

"What's a Jewish mobster? 'I'm going to break the legs of your therapist.'"
— *Richard Lewis*

"Perhaps sport should accept sponsorship from the Mafia. They kill fewer people than smoking."
— *Alan Hubbard*

"You see all these Mafia movies; Italians are always portrayed as angry, violent people. That's not right. As far as we Italians are concerned—hey, listen, we don't hurt people, but people get hurt, you know? Accidents happen! You walk outside, trip and fall on an ice pick, six or seven times, you know? Right away, they blame Vinny. That's not right."
— *Mike Ricca*

"In 1982 the body of former Vatican banker Roberto Calvi was found hanging below the Blackfriars Bridge in London. Mafia involvement is widely speculated, although to this day the Mafia claims it was simply a tragic bungee jumping gone awry."
— *Jesse James*

"When you're in California and you think about New York, right off you think about the mob. Right? You think about the mob. And when the mob wants to take somebody out, they take that guy out—that's it. Nothing to it: organized crime. In South Central, we got unorganized crime. 'Did you get him?' 'I got somebody....'"
— *Eric Blake*

CHAPTER FIVE
Interrogation Room

A well-known wise guy was picked up by police on suspicion of pistol whipping a local merchant. Several hours later he was back on the street conducting business as usual.

A rookie cop couldn't believe it. He asked the chief detective, "Didn't you give that guy the third degree?"

The detective said, "We browbeat him for three hours, shined a light in his face, and asked him hundreds of questions."

The rookie said, "You couldn't get a confession?"

The detective said, "He just kept saying, 'Yes Dear.'"

Mobsters get asked lots of questions by lots of people—cops, lawyers, judges, prosecutors, FBI agents, Congressional committees—and their standard response divulges no information. The classic answer comes from Vincent "Jimmy Blue Eyes" Alo: "According to my best recollection, I don't remember."

To say anything more would make you a rat, stool pigeon, or informer. And we know what happens to them. The lucky ones get rubbed out. The others go into witness protection and wish they were dead.

Questions also come from wives and mistresses. They get as much information as anyone else—none. Like the wise guy says, "Yes Dear."

The Italian mob calls this code of silence "Omerta." And it's a basic principle for organized crime around the world. From the Russian and Mexican Mafia to the Triads and Yakuza, loose lips sink ships and talkers end up at the bottom of the ocean too. Hey, it's just business.

In this chapter, you'll find lots of questions about life in the mob. You'll even find some answers. But if anyone asks you about it, don't forget: to the best of your recollection you don't remember.

Mob Q & A

Q: How many mobsters does it take to change a light bulb?
A: Three. One to screw it in, one to watch, and one to shoot the witness.

Q: How many mobsters does it take to change a light bulb?
A: 43. You gotta problem with that?

Q: How many goodfellas does it take to change a light bulb?
A: "Any one of youz, but not Vinnie – he's stirring the sauce."

Q: What's the difference between an insurance company actuary and a mob actuary?
A: An insurance company actuary can tell you how many people will die this year, a mob actuary can name them.

Q: What do you get when you cross the Godfather with a lawyer?
A: An offer you can't understand.

Q: Why did the mobster kill Einstein?
A: He knew too much.

Q: How many men do you need for a mob funeral?
A: Only one. To slam the car trunk shut.

Q: What do you get when you cross a mobster with a Jehovah's Witness?
A: Lots of converts.

Q: What's the one thing that keeps most mobsters out of college?
A: High school.

Q: How many mobsters does it take to open a beer?
A: None. It should be open when his wife brings it.

Q: What's the fastest way to a mobster's heart?
A: Through his chest with a sharp knife.

Q: You go to a cockfight. How do you know if an idiot is there?
A: He's the one with a duck.
Q: How do you know if a sucker is there?
A: He bet on the duck.
Q: How do you know if the Mafia is there?
A: The duck wins.

Q: What's the difference between a mob boss and God?
A: God doesn't think He's a mob boss

Q: Why do Jewish mobsters like to watch porno movies backwards?
A: They like the part where the hooker gives the money back.

Q: Who was the last person to see Jimmy Hoffa?
A: Jacques Cousteau.

Q: What do a dead mistress, a wife's anniversary, and a toilet have in common?
A: Mobsters always miss them.

Q: Why is a mobster's divorce so expensive?
A: Because it's worth it

Q: How many mobster jokes are there?
A: Three. The rest are true stories.

Q: What's the problem with mobster jokes?
A: Mobsters don't think they're funny, and everyone else thinks they're not jokes.

Q: How can you tell if a mobster's "clients" are happy with their "protection"?
A: Who cares?

I'm taking the Fifth.

Why Did the Chicken Cross the Road? (According to Mobsters)

Al Capone: What if I could guarantee it won't get to the other side?

Louis Buchalter: I don't know, but give me five minutes with the chicken and I'll find out.

John Gotti: Forget the chicken. You cross me and you're dead.

Lucky Luciano: I take the Fifth.

Bugsy Seigel: Who are you calling chicken?

Meyer Lansky: To launder money with Colonel Sanders.

Carlo Gambino: I don't remember. And no matter what you say I'm still not gonna remember.

Joseph Valachi: That's no chicken; it's a stool pigeon.

Henry Hill: To get into the witness protection program.

Sam Giancano: To have a secret meeting with John F. Kennedy.

Mickey Cohen: You tell me—or else.

Santos Trafficante Jr.: To invade Cuba.

Joe Colombo: To start a Chicken-American civil rights league.

Joe Bonanno: Cause it (censored) wanted to. That's the (censored) reason.

John Gotti Jr.: Urrrrrp. What chicken?

More Mob Q & A

Q: How many mobsters does it take to throw a man down the stairs?
A: None. He fell.

Q: How does a mobster play poker?
A: Four clubs beat a king.

Q: How does a mobster go fishing?
A: He catches one fish, then beats it until it tells him where the others are.

Q: What do you get when you cross a mobster and an exorcist?
A: Beats the hell out of me.

Q: Does the Mafia exist only in Italy and America?
A: No. It also exists in Russia, only there it's called the government.

Q: What do you call a strip bar owned by Zen mobsters?
A: The Buddha Bing.

Q: What do French mobsters fear more than anything else?
A: The quiche of death.

Q: A rapist, a gangster, and a murderer are in the same car. Who is driving the car?
A: A police officer!

Q: Did you hear about the burglar who fell in the cement mixer?
A: Now he's a hardened criminal.

Q: Detective: How did you get into counterfeiting?
A: Criminal: I answered an ad that said, "Make money at home."

Q: Why do violinists leave their instrument cases on the dashboards of their cars?
A: If someone mistakes them for Mafia, they might get some respect.

Q: What's the difference between a mobster and a pit bull?
A: Jewelry.

Q: How are mob soldiers like noodles?
A: They're always in hot water, they lack taste, and they need dough.

Q: What's an exchange of opinions at a meeting between a godfather and his capos?
A: You show up with your opinions and leave with his.

Q: What's the difference between a mob loan and a car battery?
A: The battery has a positive side.

Q: What do you get if you cross the Mafia with a herring?
A: NEVER cross the Mafia!

Q: What is the mob's plan to create thousands of small businesses?
A: Create partnerships with thousands of big businesses and wait.

Q: Why did the post office recall the new stool-pigeon stamps?
A: Because mobsters couldn't decide which side to spit on.

Q: Who would win in a fight between the Russian Mafia and the Mexican Mafia?
A: We all would.

Q: What's the difference between a loan-shark enforcer and a microwave oven?
A: A microwave stops when you open the door.

Q: What do you say to a well-dressed mob soldier?
A: Will the defendant please rise?

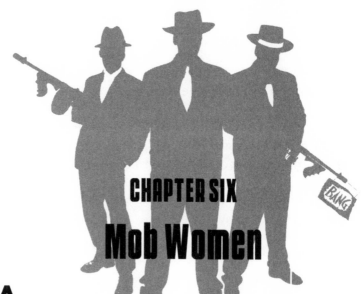

CHAPTER SIX
Mob Women

A mobster was complaining to a friend. He said, "I had it all—money, a beautiful house, a big car, the love of a beautiful woman, then... POW... it was all gone!" The friend asked, "What happened?" The mobster said, "My wife found out."

Unfortunately for the mobster, his experience was unusual. More typically, mob wives know all about the mistresses and hookers that populate their husbands' lives. It goes with the territory. And it's tolerated.

A mobster's macho magnetism that attracts women in the first place can also repel them. And if a woman—girlfriend, wife, mistress— doesn't like what he does, then tough! The world of the mob is a male-dominated, sexist culture. Women play a lot of roles but equal partner isn't one of them. Many jokes reflect this reality.

For example, mob women are expected to take care of routine household chores.

Q: How many mobsters does it take to clean a toilet?
A: None; it's a woman's job.

Mob women are also treated as sex objects often with a hint of underlying violence.

Q. How come a mobster's eyes water during sex on a first date?
A. Mace

But mobsters can also be tender and sentimental to women—especially their mothers. On May 13, 2007, the *St. Louis Post-Dispatch* ran a story about mobsters and mothers. It reported that Mothers Day was so important to mobsters that they suspended killing and racketeering for the holiday. And that the bond between mobsters and their mothers is "more sacred than the oath of Omerta."

In this chapter you will find humor that expresses the special relationship between mobsters and their women.

Wise-Guy Wisdom on Love and Sex

Love is a delusion that one woman differs from another.

Sex is a three-letter word that needs some old-fashioned four-letter words to convey it's full meaning.

Virginity can be cured.

Never sleep with anyone crazier than yourself.

Sex is dirty only if it's done right.

A hard-on doesn't count as personal growth.

Sex is not the answer. Sex is the question—YES is the answer.

You may get off on a cheap hooker but you can't get off on a cheap lawyer.

Women are like guns; keep one around long enough and you're going to want to shoot it.

Sex is always a great birthday gift.

A sense of humor doesn't mean she tells jokes; it means she laughs at yours.

You don't pay for sex. You pay her to leave after you're done.

Things that Wise Guys Wished Their Girlfriends Knew

Learn to work the toilet seat: if it's up, put it down yourself.

Don't rub the lamp if you don't want the genie to come out.

If you think you're fat, you probably are. Don't ask us.

Don't ask what we're thinking about unless you want to discuss sex, sports or cars.

Anyone can buy condoms.

Yes, pissing standing up is more difficult than peeing from point blank range. We're bound to miss sometimes.

If you don't dress like a Victoria's Secret girl, don't expect us to act like a soap-opera guy.

Christopher Columbus didn't need directions, and neither do we.

If we offer help while you're getting ready, it means you're late.

If we hear from an old girlfriend we will fantasize about having sex with her. But don't worry; the fantasy includes you too.

Men are from Earth; women are from Earth. Deal with it.

Mobster Pick-Up Lines

Are you free tonight or will it cost me?

Even if you were a fish I'd want to sleep with you.

You remind me of my dead ex-girlfriend.

If looks could kill, you'd get 25 to life.

Interested in serving HARD time?

That's a gun in my pocket and I am happy to see you.

Headline Hits: Mob Women

Luchese Mob Wife Is 'Moll'ified
(*New York Post*, December 22, 2007)

"The wife and high-school sweetheart of a jailed Luchese mobster remains loyal to her man despite his alleged recent affair with a hotshot Hollywood producer."

Whack-a-Moll—
Vinny Wanted to Kill My Gal: Rat
(*New York Post*, June 29, 2007)

"Former Bonanno captain Dominick Cicale said yesterday his boss, Vincent 'Vinny Gorgeous' Basciano, wanted Cicale's girlfriend whacked after [Vincent Basciano] found out she'd tattled to his wife that he sired a child with another woman—getting the mob boss kicked out of his own house."

Mobster a Breast Friend
(*New York Post*, May 22, 2003)

"The former DeCavalcante acting boss, who made at least $2 million out of his Rego Park sex joint, Wiggles, claimed he revolutionized the sex business by making his dancers 'partners' in the club."

Mob Mistress 'Checks Out' – Body Found in L.I. Motel Room

(*New York Post*, April 1, 2004)

"The mistress of Gambino mob boss Peter Gotti was found dead yesterday less than a week after she vaulted to fame as the mobster's moll, police said.

"Marjorie Alexander was found fully clothed with a plastic bag over her head—duct-taped around her neck—at a Red Roof Inn in Westbury, L.I., yesterday afternoon."

Stand by Your Made Man? Wife Bails – and Tells All

(*Daily News*, New York, July 10th 2006)

"You've seen the breakups and makeups of Tony and Carmela Soprano. But, when it comes to romantic fury, the TV mob couple has nothing on Joe and Nancy Defede.

"The Defedes are the real deal. For four years, Joe was acting boss of the Lucchese crime family—until 1998, when he pleaded guilty to shaking down garment businesses. He and Nancy have been married for 35 years (the last three in the federal witness protection program).

"Living in close quarters under assumed names in a state far from Howard Beach has been the kiss of death for their romance.

"'I've had enough,' Nancy tells us. 'It's not a life.'

"Their impending split isn't stopping them from collaborating on what may be the first memoir of a Mafia marriage.

"'She's the writer,' says Joe, 72. 'I'll help where I can. I don't want to hold her back. I dragged her through all this, and she stuck with me.'"

Feds Say Hers Was a Love to Die For

(*Daily News*, New York, May 31, 1995)

"CAROL LUCANIA COULD BE the ultimate mob moll.

"She'll entice your victim to her home, let you use the place to beat him to death, help clean up the bloody mess and, once you've gotten rid of the body, cook dinner for you and your mob associates.

"That's what Lucania did when her paramour of the moment, Anthony Persichetti, wanted to kill off the 49-year-old Bensonhurst woman's previous lover, according to FBI agent Peter Kohn."

Turncoat Mobster a Wives-Guy— Gal Pal a Mafia Spouse

(*New York Post*, April 24, 2004)

"A mob turncoat who has violated the oath of silence to testify against two men who allegedly shot him now admits he may have broken another Mafia code—the one that makes other wise guy's wives off-limits.

"For months after he was shot in Coney Island on July 16, 2001, former Colombo wise guy Joseph Campanella adamantly refused to reveal to authorities the identity of the triggerman.

"But he went out of his way to make a reassuring call to a former girlfriend—who was married to a Gambino crime-family associate."

Mob Women Q & A

Q: What do you do with a 40-year-old mistress who thinks she's God's gift?
A: Trade her in for two 20-year-olds.

Q: What do you call a mob wife who knows where her husband is every night?
A: A widow.

Q: Why do mobsters find it difficult to make eye contact in a nightclub?
A: Breasts don't have eyes.

Q: What's the difference between a wife and a mistress?
A: About 45 pounds.

Q: What is a mobster's view of safe sex?
A: A padded headboard.

Q: Why is a fat mistress like a moped?
A: They're both fun to ride until your friends see you with one.

Q: What are three words mobsters hate to hear when having sex?
A: "Honey, I'm home!"

Q: Why do mobsters come home drunk and leave their clothes on the floor?
A: Because they're in them.

Q: What does a mobster have that's six inches long, two inches wide and gets a mistress excited?
A: Money.

Q: Why do mistresses fake orgasms?
A: They think mobsters care.

Q: What's the definition of making love?
A: Something a mistress does while a mobster is screwing her.

Q: What do you call a wise guy who expects sex on a second date?
A: Slow.

Q: What's a mobster's idea of honesty in a relationship?
A: Telling you his real name.

Q: Why do all mobsters like smart mistresses?
A: They're better at doing the dishes.

Q: Why did the mistress call her mobster "Snowstorm"?
A: Because she never knew when he was coming, how many inches she'd get, or how long he'd stay.

Q: What do mobsters enjoy even more than lots of sex?
A: Talking to their buddies about it.

Q: How can a mob wife tell if her husband is dead?
A: The sex is the same, but she gets the remote.

Q: Why do you tend not to ask out the chick at the bar with the black eye?
A: Because you already know the bitch doesn't listen.

Q: Why do mobsters think air is like sex?
A: It's no big deal unless they're not getting any.

Q: What do you call a mobster without a mistress?
A: A liar.

Q: What do you do when your dishwasher stops?
A: Kick her in the ass!

Q: What kind of jewelry does a mobster look best in?
A: Handcuffs.

Q: What do you say to a mob thug with a good-looking girl on his arm?
A: Nice tattoo.

Q: Why do mob mistresses wear underwear?
A: To keep their ankles warm.

The first guy taken for a ride.

The New Mistress

Mobster 1: I hear you just got a new mistress.

Mobster 2: Yeah, it's the fourth one in a year.

Mobster 1: What happened to the first three?

Mobster 2: They all died.

Mobster 1: How did that happen?

Mobster 2: The first one ate poison mushrooms.

Mobster 1: And the second?

Mobster 2: She ate poison mushrooms.

Mobster 1: And the third ate poison mushrooms too?

Mobster 2: No. She died of a broken neck.

Mobster 1: Really?

Mobster 2: Yeah. She wouldn't eat the mushrooms.

Top 10 Reasons Why Handguns Are Better than Women

#10. You can trade an old 44 for a new 22.

#9. You can keep one handgun at home and have another for when you're on the road.

#8. If you admire a friend's handgun and tell him so, he will probably let you try it out a few times.

#7. Your primary handgun doesn't mind if you keep another handgun for a backup.

#6. Your handgun will stay with you even if you run out of ammo.

#5. A handgun doesn't take up a lot of closet space.

#4. Handguns function normally every day of the month.

#3. A handgun doesn't ask, "Do these new grips make me look fat?"

#2. A handgun doesn't mind if you go to sleep after you use it.

And the number one reason a handgun is favored over a woman

#1. YOU CAN BUY A SILENCER FOR A HANDGUN.

You Can't Make this Stuff Up

Sperm Smuggling

On December 4, 2002, the Associated Press reported that Kevin Granato, a hit man for the Columbo crime family, and his wife were indicted on a charge of criminal conspiracy for smuggling sperm out of Allenwood Federal Prison in Pennsylvania. He was one of five New York mobsters believed to have smuggled sperm out of the prison in order to impregnate their wives.

It could give a whole new meaning to hot goods.

Artificial Insemination

On July 7, 2006 AHN Media reported that an Italian judge ruled that a jailed Mafia boss should be allowed to pursue fatherhood through artificial insemination. Salvio Madonia, who is serving a life sentence for murder, is not allowed to see his wife. So the judge ruled that Italy's public health service must pay for an official to go to Madonia's prison and collect his sperm.

So they can't snuggle but they don't have to smuggle. (And what exactly does the ruling mean by "collect his sperm"?)

Two-Timing Mistress

On May 6, 1997, *The Sun* of London, England reported that a Mafia chief kidnapped his two-timing mistress and her new lover. Then he had them thrown down a shaft leading to a cavern under a mountain. At the bottom of the shaft were eight starving dogs, including pit bulls, that ate the couple.

So the Mafia chief and his mistress both got shafted. That's the danger of beauty. If the mistress had been a dog, she wouldn't have been fed to one.

Viagra Vendetta

On May 6, 2005, the *Associated Press* reported that three physicians in a suburb of New York City were accused of supplying Viagra to members of the Gambino crime family. After arraignment in U.S. District Court in Manhattan, they were freed on $50,000 bail each. A lawyer for one said, "These are hard working, honest doctors. Apparently, I guess the rule is that if you're alleged to be a wise guy, don't get sick." However, Viagra and other drugs were prescribed so frequently that one of the doctors jokes he was part of the family. And in a secretly recorded conversation, one doctor referred to himself as the medical "consigliere" to the family.

When these mobsters talk about stiffs it's not always a corpse.

CHAPTER SEVEN
The Mob Goes to the Movies

On February 22, 2008, the *New York Post* reported that during a sentencing in federal court, mob killer Francesco Fiordilini blamed Hollywood for turning him into a stereotypical Mafia wise guy. He said, "Although I made all my drastic decisions on my own, Hollywood intensified my love for that life and in the process blindsided what being Italian meant." In other words, movies mobbed him up. (Now the authorities better make sure he doesn't watch *Escape From Alcatraz*.)

Do movies really have that kind of power? Who knows? But you don't have to worry about the ones listed in this chapter. Although they involve gangsters, mobsters, racketeers and other denizens of organized crime, they all have funny plots—either main, sub or burial. In fact, this is one of the most comprehensive lists of mob-related comedies ever assembled. So enjoy it. Or else.

Movies

8 Heads in a Duffel Bag (1997)
A wise guy hired to bring a bag of victims' heads to a crime boss gets into trouble when the bag accidentally gets switched with a tourist's luggage.
Cast Includes: Joe Pesci, David Spade

99 and 44/100% Dead (1974)
A mobster hires a hit man to kill his rival in a gang war.
Cast Includes: Richard Harris, Edmund O'Brien

A Good Night to Die (2003)
One hit man tries to save the life of another hit man who has become a problem for the bosses.
Cast Includes: Michael Rapaport, Seymour Cassel, Lainie Kazan

A Slight Case of Murder (1938)
A former bootlegger who goes legitimate has problems when his beer tastes awful and his daughter starts dating a police officer.
Cast Includes: Edward G. Robinson

The Adventures of Pluto Nash (2002)
A man who owns a nightclub on the moon tries to keep mobsters from taking it over.
Cast Includes: Eddie Murphy, Randy Quaid

Advertising for the Mob (2008)
An incompetent ad man fired from multiple advertising agencies starts his own crime family.
Cast Includes: Victoria Babu

The All Together (2007)
After a TV producer selling his house asks his flat mate to let anyone in to look at it, the flat mate allows gangsters to enter.
Cast Includes: Martin Freeman

Almost Made (2004)
Five wannabe wise guys form their own "family" and learn being mobsters isn't as easy as they thought.
Cast Includes: Red West

American Cousins (2007)
Two American mobsters posing as PR consultants hide out in a Glasgow Café owned by their cousin.
Cast Includes: Dan Hedaya

Analyze This (1999)
A mob boss suffering from anxiety attacks complicates the life of a psychiatrist by seeking a cure before a major meeting of Mafia leaders.
Cast Includes: Robert De Niro, Billy Crystal, Lisa Kudrow

Analyze That (2002)
Mob boss fakes insanity to get out of prison, resumes therapy with his analyst and tries to go straight with great difficulty. Sequel to *Analyze This*.
Cast Includes: Robert De Niro, Billy Crystal, Lisa Kudrow

Angels Dance (1999)
A novice hit man is trained by an offbeat expert and then required to kill a woman randomly picked out of the phone book.
Cast Includes: James Belushi

Another Face (1935)
A mobster from New York gets his face changed, kills the doctor who changed it, moves to Hollywood and tries to get into movies.
Cast Includes: Brian Donlevy, Wallace Ford, Alan Hale

Any Which Way You Can (1980)

A fighter who wants to retire is forced by the Mafia to fight one more time.

Cast Includes: Clint Eastwood

Avenging Angelo (2002)

The daughter of a mob boss killed by a hit man seeks revenge and is helped by the boss' bodyguard.

Cast Includes: Sylvester Stallone, Madeleine Stowe

Mob Chess

Baby Face Morgan (1942)

When the head of an insurance business dies, his associates get his son to run the business even though the son doesn't know his father was a mob leader and the business is a front.

Cast Includes: Richard Cromwell, Mary Carlisle, Robert Armstrong

The Baby Juice Express (2004)

When an imprisoned mobster tries to smuggle his sperm to his wife, it gets hijacked and held for ransom.

Cast Includes: Nick Brimble

Baby on Board (1991)

Widow of a mob bookkeeper gets help from a cabdriver as she and her daughter flee from a hit man.

Cast Includes: Carol Kane, Judge Rheinhold

Bad Apple (2004 TV)

Complications ensue when an FBI undercover agent who has infiltrated a mob loan-sharking operation is attracted to his informant's sister.

Cast Includes: Chris Noth, Mercedes Ruehl

Ball of Fire (1941)

A group of professors writing a dictionary of slang find the perfect source in a mob moll and they help her escape from her gangster boyfriend.

Cast Includes: Gary Cooper, Barbara Stanwyck, Dana Andrews, Dan Duryea

Be Cool (2005)

Former mobster exits movie business and enters music business, but still uses skills he learned as a mobster. Sequel to *Get Shorty*.

Cast Includes: John Travolta, Uma Thurman

The Big Hit (1998)

Problems occur when a hit man and his crew kidnap a woman who turns out to be the god-daughter of their boss—and the hit man falls in love with her.

Cast Includes: Mark Wahlberg, Lou Diamond Phillips, Christina Applegate

Big Money Hustlas (2000 video)

The New York Police Department sends for a quirky San Francisco supercop to help battle a crime lord.

Cast Includes: Harland Williams

The Big Shot (1937)

A veterinarian uses millions of dollars inherited from his uncle to lead a crusade against crime in the small town where his uncle, unbeknownst to him, was the crime boss.

Cast Includes: Guy Kibbee

The Big Slice (1991)

Two guys, who write unpublished books together and support themselves by driving a cab and working in a pizza place, get exciting new writing material when a dead body that turns up in the cab leads to entanglements with the mob.

Cast Includes: Heather Locklear

The Biggest Bundle of Them All (1968)

An American mobster gets revenge when his friends won't pay any ransom after he's kidnapped by inept European mobsters.

Cast Includes: Vittorio De Sica, Raquel Welch, Robert Wagner

Black Belt Jones (1974)

When a karate school owner is killed by a mobster, his daughter and one of his star pupils kick some mob butt.

Cast Includes: Jim Kelly, Scatman Cruthers

Blame It On the Bellboy (1992)
After a hotel bellboy mixes up messages, a hit man goes to kill a woman from a dating agency and a real estate agent goes to buy property from gangsters—among other mix-ups.
Cast Includes: Dudley Moore

Body Trouble (1992)
A screenwriter gets involved with a jealous mobster and his beautiful girlfriend.
Cast Includes: Dick Van Patten, Frank Gorshin

Blonde and Blonder (2007)
Two dumb blondes are mistaken for hit men by both the Mafia and the FBI.
Cast Includes: Pamela Anderson, Denise Richards

Bookies (2003)
College buddies become bookies and attract attention from the mob when they get too greedy.
Cast Includes: Nick Stahl, Lukas Haas

Bring Me the Head of Mavis Davis (1997)
Manager plans to kill pop star client in order to increase album sales.
Cast Includes: Danny Aiello

Broadway Danny Rose (1984)
After a talent agent helps a singer by posing as the boyfriend of the singer's mistress, two mobsters come after the talent agent.
Cast Includes: Woody Allen, Mia Farrow

Brother Orchid (1940)
A mob boss returns from Europe to find his old gang taken over by another mobster, forms a rival gang, gets wounded and joins a monastery.
Cast Includes: Edward G. Robinson, Humphrey Bogart, Ann Sothern

Buddy, Buddy (1981)

A hit man on his way to kill a mobster becomes entangled in the affairs of a depressed man he meets en route to the job.

Cast Includes: Jack Lemmon, Walter Matthau, Paula Prentiss

Bugsy Malone (1976)

A musical gangster story set in 1929 New York features child actors in all the parts.

Cast Includes: Jodie Foster, Scott Baio

Bullets Over Broadway (1994)

In order to get his play produced, an idealistic playwright must cast a mobster's bimbo girlfriend in a key role.

Cast Includes: John Cusack, Dianne Wiest, Chazz Palminteri, Jennifer Tilly

The Busy Body (1967)

The goofy assistant to a mob boss is accused of stealing mob money and tries to clear himself by finding a corpse buried in a suit containing the stolen money.

Cast Includes: Sid Caesar, Robert Ryan, Anne Baxter

Buy Me That Town (1941)

Big-city gangsters buy a small town to use as a hideout, become involved with the locals and change their attitude about crime.

Cast Includes: Lloyd Nolan, Constance Moore, Sheldon Leonard

Chow Bella (1998)

A crime reporter turned food critic has problems after he gives a bad review to a restaurant owned by the mob.

Cast Includes: Clint Howard

Coldblooded (1995)

After falling in love, a mob bookie promoted to hit man must find a way to leave the mob.

Cast Includes: Jason Priestly

Cookie (1989)

When a gangster gets out of prison, he finds the best way to get reacquainted with his illegitimate daughter is to hire her as his chauffeur.

Cast Includes: Peter Falk, Diane Weist

Corky Romano (2001)

The veterinarian son of a mob boss infiltrates the FBI to get rid of evidence about his father.

Cast Includes: Chris Kattan, Peter Falk

Crashing Hollywood (1938)

After an ex-con and two screenwriters make a successful gangster movie, the gangster who inspired it is not happy.

Cast Includes: Paul Guilfoyle

The Crew (2000)

In order to save their retirement home, four retired mobsters plan one last job.

Cast Includes: Burt Reynolds, Seymour Cassel, Richard Dreyfuss, Dan Hedaya

Crime Spree (2003)

Dumb burglars from France mistakenly rob a house in Chicago that belongs to the head of the Chicago mob.

Cast Includes: Harvey Keitel, Gerard Depardieu

Crooked Lines (2003)

Some wise guys plan to rob a mob-operated deli of a million dollars on the last day of February but forget to account for leap year.

Cast Includes: Burt Young, Anne Meara, Colin Quin

Day at the Beach (1998)

After accidentally killing someone, a low-level worker at a New York ravioli factory discovers that the factory is a front for the mob and falls in love while evading mobsters.

Cast Includes: Jane Adams

Dead Fish (2005)

The lives of several people, including a hit man and a loan shark, become comically interconnected after two cell phones get switched by mistake.

Cast Includes: Gary Oldman, Terrence Stamp

Dead Lenny (2006)

After a mob underling transporting $5 million from Los Angeles disappears, a mobster sends his minions to find him – and the money.

Cast Includes: John Heard, Nicole Eggert, Joe Piscopo

Dinner Rush (2000)

Tonight's guests at a restaurant owned by a mobster include a police detective, a famous food critic, and rival mobsters who want to become "partners" in the restaurant.

Cast Includes: Danny Aiello

Dirty Deeds (2002)

The profitable operations of an Australian mobster who controls gambling in Sydney attracts the attention of the American Mafia.

Cast Includes: John Goodman, Toni Collette

Every Little Crook and Nanny (1972)

A dancing school teacher kidnaps the son of a mob boss after his gang turns her school into a gambling operation.

Cast Includes: Lynn Redgrave, Victor Mature

Everybody's Doing It (1938)

A man fired from an advertising agency starts a puzzle contest with a $200,000 prize that attracts the attention of gangsters.

Cast Includes: Preston Foster

F– Man (1936)

After a soda-jerk pesters government agents for a job as a G-Man, he's given the fake title F-Man and becomes unwittingly involved with a mobster and his moll.

Cast Includes: Jack Haley, William Frawley

The Fall Guy (1930)

After an inept druggist loses his job, he gets set-up by a gangster trafficking in illegal drugs.

Cast Includes: Mae Clarke

Find Me Guilty (2006)

A mobster defends himself in court rather than using a lawyer or accepting a plea deal to rat out his friends.

Cast Includes: Vin Diesel

Forget About It (2006)

Unaware that cash they found in the desert belongs to the mob, three retirees live it up until the mob and FBI come after them.

Cast Includes: Burt Reynolds, Robert Loggia, Raquel Welch, Charles Durning

The Freshman (1990)

A film student gets involved with a mobster who imports exotic animals for a gourmet restaurant.

Cast Includes: Marlon Brando, Matthew Broderick, Penelope Ann Miller

Friends and Family (2001)

A gay couple who are Mafia hit men must keep their occupation secret when one of the couple's mother and FBI agent father come for a visit.

Cast Includes: Tony Lo Bianco, Anna Maria Alberghetti

Frogs for Snakes (1998)

A loan shark who owns an Off-Broadway theater uses unemployed actors as debt collectors in exchange for getting them roles in plays in his theater.

Cast Includes: Robbie Coltrane, Harry Hamlin

Fugitive Lovers (1934)

A New York chorus girl gets on a bus to Los Angeles to flee from an overly romantic racketeer who boards the bus too and gets upset when the girl gets lovey-dovey with another passenger, an escaped convict.

Cast Includes: Robert Montgomery, Ted Healy

Funland (1987)

A clown fired after the mob takes over an amusement park seeks revenge.

Cast Includes: William Windom

The Gang Buster (1931)

A small-town insurance agent bumbles his way into a mob war.

Cast Includes: Jack Oakie, Jean Arthur

The Gang That Couldn't Shoot Straight (1971)

Two warring Mafia families use unorthodox techniques to fight each other.

Cast Includes: Jerry Orbach, Robert De Niro, Hervé Villechaize

Gangster Exchange (2010)

A Yakuza from Tokyo and an enforcer from the Bosnian mob race around New York City after stealing a 50-pound toilet made of heroin in the middle of a mob war.

Cast Includes: Christopher Russell

The Gay Bride (1934)
A gold digger marries and becomes widowed to a succession of gangsters.
Cast Includes: Carole Lombard, Zasu Pitts

Get Shorty (1995)
A Miami mobster goes to Hollywood to collect a debt and finds that his mobster skills work well for a new job—movie producer.
Cast Includes: John Travolta, Gene Hackman, Rene Russo

Gigli (2003)
After the mob orders an inept hit man to kidnap the mentally challenged brother of a federal prosecutor, a lesbian gangster is sent to oversee the operation and they fall in love.
Cast Includes: Ben Affleck, Jennifer Lopez

Glitch (1988)
After robbing a house, two thieves mistaken for the owners decide to stay for a party not knowing that the real owners owe money to gangsters.
Cast Includes: Dick Gautier

The Godson (1998)
The patriarch of a crime family sends his son to Mafia University to learn how to run the family business but rival crime families are ready to take over.
Cast Includes: Rodney Dangerfield, Dom Deluise, Kevin McDonald

The Golden Fleecing (1940)
An insurance salesman gets entangled with gangsters.
Cast Includes: Lew Ayres, Virginia Grey, Nat Pendleton

Gun Shy (2000)
A DEA agent in mortal fear of a Mafia boss and on the verge of a mental breakdown must complete one last covert operation so he seeks psychiatric help from a therapy group.
Cast Includes: Liam Neeson, Sandra Bullock, Oliver Platt

Half a Sinner (1940)
A schoolteacher seeking adventure hooks up with a gangster, steals his car with a corpse in the trunk, gets pursued by the gangster and police, and finds romance.
Cast Includes: Heather Angel

The Happening (1967)
A retired mob boss is kidnapped and held for ransom by a group of hippies.
Cast Includes: Anthony Quinn, Faye Dunaway, Milton Berle

Harlem Nights (1989)
Owner of an illegal gambling operation must defend himself against police and other gangsters in the era of the Harlem renaissance.
Cast Includes: Eddie Murphy, Richard Pryor, Red Foxx

Harvard Man (2001)
A Harvard student trying to help his parents borrows money from his girlfriend's mobster father and gets entangled in fixing a basketball game.
Cast Includes: Sarah Michelle Gellar

He Laughed Last (1956)
A show girl becomes a mob boss.
Cast Includes: Frankie Laine, Jesse White

Hide Out (1934)

An injured racketeer hiding out in a farmhouse falls in love with a country girl.

Cast Includes: Edward Arnold, Robert Montgomery, Maureen O'Sullivan

Hideaway (1937)

A small-town bumbler and his family living in an abandoned house meet the people who abandoned it—gangsters who want to use it as a hideout.

Cast Includes: Fred Stone, Marjorie Lord

Hiding Out (1987)

A stockbroker who will testify against a mobster hides out as a student in a high school because of death threats.

Cast Includes: Jon Cryer, Annabeth Gish

High Times Potluck (2002)

A mobster discovers the wonders of marijuana.

Cast Includes: Frank Gorshin

The Hit (1984)

Two inept hit men must escort an ex-mobster from Spain to Paris.

Cast Includes: John Hurt, Tim Roth, Terence Stamp

Hollow Point (1996)

A female FBI agent and a macho DEA agent are forced to team up to stop a crime lord trying to merge Russian, Chinese and Italian gangsters into one group.

Cast Includes: John Lithgow, Donald Sutherland

Hollywood & Wine (2010)

A man in debt to a mobster attracted to a movie star convinces his girlfriend to pose as the star and have dinner with the mobster in order to cancel the debt.

Cast Includes: Pamela Anderson, Vivica A. Fox, Chris Kattan

Hoodlum & Son (2003)

A reluctant mobster indebted to a mob boss plans to rob a speakeasy but things go astray when his young son wanders in and they both flee to a dustbowl town.

Cast Includes: Ron Perlman, Robert Vaughn

Hoods (1998)

A mobster orders six people to kill an enemy who bombed his building, but the enemy turns out to be a nine-year-old.

Cast Includes: Joe Mantegna

I Can't Give You Anything But Love, Baby (1940)

A mobster forces a man to set a poem to music and then gets the song on "The Hit Parade."

Cast Includes: Broderick Crawford

I Went Down (1997)

After a man harms a mobster trying to collect a debt, the mobster's mob boss uncle pairs the man with a dim-wit mobster and orders them to bring yet another mobster from Cork to Dublin.

Cast Includes: Brendan Gleason

I Work for Johnny (2007)

After accidentally rear-ending a mobster's car, an average Joe ends up in the middle of a mob war.

Cast Includes: Jim Galloway

In Bruges (2008)

Two Irish hit men are ordered to lay low in a Belgian town after they bungle a shooting back home.

Cast Includes: Colin Farrell, Ralph Fiennes

In the Mix (2005)

A DJ hired by a mob boss as the bodyguard for his daughter gets in the middle of mob activity.

Cast Includes: Usher, Chazz Palminteri

Innocent Blood (1992)

A mobster bitten by a vampire begins a crime family of vampires while the vampire who bit him tries to stop him.

Cast Includes: Tony Sirrico, Robert Loggia

Invitation to a Suicide (2004)

A young man sells tickets to his suicide so he can pay back a mobster who has threatened to kill his father.

Cast Includes: Pablo Schreiber

Island of Love (1963)

After two con-men go to Greece to escape a gangster who financed their movie flop, one falls in love with the gangster's niece as they plot additional scams.

Cast Includes: Robert Preston, Tony Randall, Walter Matthau

Izzy & Moe (1985 TV)

Based on a true story, two retired vaudevillians become prohibition agents and use their theatrical skills to nab mobsters.

Cast Includes: Jackie Gleason, Art Carney

The Jerky Boys (1995)

Trouble ensues when two telephone pranksters try to impress New York mobsters by impersonating a Chicago crime boss.

Cast Includes: John G. Brennan, Kamal Ahmed, Alan Arkin, Vincent Pastore

Jerry and Tom (1998)

A veteran hit man and a novice hit man who both work at a used car lot have different attitudes to their mob enforcement duties.

Cast Includes: Joe Mantegna, Sam Rockwell, Ted Danson

Johnny Slade's Greatest Hits (2005) (aka Meet The Mobsters)

A mob boss in hiding gives orders through the songs sung by a down-and-out lounge singer he arranged to have hired at a hot night club.

Cast Includes: John Fiore

Kangaroo Jack (2003)

Two friends from New York, delivering mob money to Australia, have problems when a wild kangaroo gets the money by accident.

Cast Includes: Christopher Walken, Dyan Cannon

Kansas City Princess (1934)

Two manicurists flee Kansas City to get away from a gangster.

Cast Includes: Joan Blondell, Robert Armstrong

Killer Dill (1947)

A salesman who is an exact double for a mob hit man gets into comic adventures.

Cast Includes: Stuart Erwin, Frank Albertson

Killer per caso (1997) (aka The Good Bad Guy)

After being hired by a mobster to kill a witness, an Italian immigrant disguises himself as a cop to do the job; but he must enforce the law when he's mistaken for a real police officer.

Cast Includes: Dom DeLuise, Ronnie Schell

Knockaround Guys (2001)

After the delivery of a bag of cash goes awry, the sons of four New York mobsters team up to retrieve it from a small town in Montana.

Cast Includes: Dennis Hopper, Vin Diesel, John Malkovich

The Lady and the Mob (1939)

A society woman assembles a gang of big-city mobsters to fight the racketeers exploiting her small town.

Cast Includes: Fay Bainter, Ida Lupino, Henry Armetta

Lady Scarface (1941)

A police officer pursues a Chicago gang unaware that its leader is a woman.

Cast Includes: Judith Anderson

The Last Days of Frankie the Fly (1997)

A flunky who works for the mob falls in love with an actress and tries to prevent her from succumbing to mob influence.

Cast Includes: Dennis Hopper, Daryl Hannah, Keifer Sutherland

The Last Godfather (2011)

A mob boss trains his illegitimate, mentally-disabled Korean son to take over the family business.

Cast Includes: Harvey Keitel, John Pinette

The Last Shot (2004)

The FBI creates a sting for a mob boss by funding a feature film for a wannabe director without telling him the movie isn't really supposed to get made.

Cast Includes: Matthew Broderick, Alec Baldwin, Toni Collette

The Lemon Drop Kid (1951)

A racetrack tout steers a gangster's girlfriend from a winning bet at a horse race and must come up with $10,000 to make up for it.

Cast Includes: Bob Hope, Marilyn Maxwell

Let's Do It Again (1975)

After two workers from Atlanta win money from gangsters in New Orleans by rigging a fight, the gangsters want their money back through another rigged fight—or else.

Cast Includes: Bill Cosby, Sidney Poitier

Life with Blondie (1945)
A gangster kidnaps the Bumsteads' dog who has become famous in advertisements after being selected as the Navy's "Pin-up Pooch."
Cast Includes: Penny Singleton, Arthur Lake

Life Without Dick (2002)
After a woman kills her boyfriend, the hit man who was supposed to kill him (and has never killed anyone before) helps her dispose of the body if she'll carry out his other assignments.
Cast Includes: Sarah Jessica Parker, Harry Connick Jr., Johnny Knoxville

The Little Giant (1933)
As prohibition ends, a bootlegger trying to break into California society purchases phony stock from a society big-wig and turns to the Chicago mob for help.
Cast Includes: Edward G. Robinson, Mary Astor

Love, Honor and Obey (2000)
A courier gets into a North London crime gang run by his friend's uncle and inadvertently starts a war with the South London mob.
Cast Includes: Jude Law, Sadie Frost

Love That Brute (1950)
A Chicago crime boss fakes that he has kids in order to hire a woman he likes as a nanny, but keeping her in the dark about his occupation is tough, especially with mobsters living in his house.
Cast Includes: Paul Douglas, Jean Peters, Cesar Romero, Joan Davis

Lucky Jordan (1942)
A racketeer drafted into the U.S. army deserts by taking a WAC hostage only to find that his old crew is selling the mob's services to enemy agents.
Cast Includes: Alan Ladd, Sheldon Leonard

Lucky Legs (1942)

After a chorus girl inherits $1,000,000, she uses it to back a Broadway show, but mobsters interfere.

Cast Includes: Jinx Falkenburg

The Lucky Stiff (1949)

A lawyer, investigating a protection racket, is attracted to a night-club singer and investigates the murder of her boss after she's sentenced to death for the crime.

Cast Includes: Dorothy Lamour, Clair Trevor

Mad Dog and Glory (1993)

A mobster rescued by a shy cop returns the favor by introducing the cop to one of his beautiful female employees.

Cast Includes: Robert De Niro, Uma Thurman, Bill Murray

Mad Dog Time (1996)

When a mob boss returns from a stay in an insane asylum, he finds that his girlfriend is having an affair with one of his underlings and rival mob bosses want to take over his territory.

Cast Includes: Ellen Barkin, Jeff Goldblum, Burt Reynolds

Made (2001)

Things go awry when a struggling boxer and his friend are engaged to deliver laundered money for a group of mobsters.

Cast Includes: Jon Favreau, Vince Vaughn, Famke Janssen

Mafia! (1998) (aka Jane Austen's Mafia!)

Spoof of *The Godfather*, *Casino*, and other Mafia movies.

Cast Includes: Jay Mohr, Lloyd Bridges, Olympia Dukakis, Christina Applegate

Mafioso (1962)

A factory worker in Northern Italy vacations with his family in Sicily so he can show them his hometown and dispel negative stereotypes about Sicilians and the Mafia.

Cast Includes: Alberto Sordi

Mail Order Bride (2003)

A mob boss sends his nephew to Moscow to bring back a Russian mail-order bride who has scammed several of his crew, but the nephew gets scammed himself.

Cast Includes: Danny Aiello, Vincent Pastore

Mambo Café (2000)

A failing restaurant hopes to gain notoriety and customers when the owner's kids invite a mobster to hang out there.

Cast Includes: Danny Aiello, Paul Rodriguez

Married to the Mob (1988)

The widow of a mobster is romantically pursued by both an FBI agent and a mob boss.

Cast Includes: Michelle Pfeiffer, Matthew Modine, Alec Baldwin

The Matador (2005)

A hit man going through a midlife crisis becomes friends with a beleaguered businessman after they meet in a bar in Mexico.

Cast Includes: Pierce Brosnan, Greg Kinnear

The Mexican (2001)

After a mob boss orders a man to go to Mexico to get an antique gun or else, his girlfriend, who wants him to leave the mob, is held hostage.

Cast Includes: Brad Pitt, Julia Roberts

Mickey Blue Eyes (1999)

A debonair British auctioneer gets engaged to the daughter of a mob boss and gets sucked into the family business.

Cast Includes: Hugh Grant, James Caan, Jeanne Tripplehorn

Midnight Run (1988)

A bounty hunter must escort a bail-jumping Mafia accountant from New York to Los Angeles while fending off attempts by the Mafia, FBI and another bounty hunter to interfere with him and his prisoner.

Cast Includes: Robert DeNiro, Charles Grodin, Yaphet Kotto

Mob Boss (1990 video)

A mob boss trains his inept son to take over both his business and romantic affairs.

Cast Includes: Morgan Fairchild, Eddie Deezen, William Hickey

Mob Queen (1998)

Low-level wise guys hire a prostitute for their boss who falls in love with her, but it turns out she is really a he—a secret that could get them killed.

Cast Includes: Tony Sirico

Mob Story (1989)

A New York gangster is forced to hide out in the small town where he was raised.

Cast Includes: Margot Kidder

Mobsters and Mormons (2005)

Culture shock ensues when the witness protection program moves a Mafia family from New Jersey to Utah.

Cast Includes: Mark DeCarlo, Britani Bateman

Money from Home (1953)
Hijinx ensue when a gambler in debt to the mob tricks his assistant veterinarian cousin into fixing a horse race.
Cast Includes: Jerry Lewis, Dean Martin

Montana (1998)
A professional hit woman assigned to find her boss' mistress is targeted by her own crime family after the mistress commits a murder.
Cast Includes: Kyra Segwick, Stanley Tucci, Robbie Coltrane

More Dogs than Bones (2000)
After a female mobster hides $1,000,000 in the bag of someone going to visit his nephew, she sends her crew to retrieve the money but the nephew's dog gets it first.
Cast Includes: Joe Mantegna, Peter Coyote, Mercedes Rule

My Blue Heaven (1990)
A mobster in the witness protection program can't keep a low profile; this is a big problem for the FBI agent who must keep him alive and out of prison.
Cast Includes: Steve Martin, Rick Moranis, Joan Cusack

Never a Dull Moment (1968)
An actor practicing a role is mistaken for a killer and must keep up the act after a gangster brings him to his lair to use him for a job.
Cast Includes: Dick Van Dyke, Edward G. Robinson, Dorothy Provine

Not Now Darling (1973)
This is a British farce about deals between a fur-salon owner and mobsters involving mistresses and fur coats.
Cast Includes: Geraldine Gardner, Leslie Phillips

Nuns On the Run (1990)

Two guys on the run from both their mobster boss and local Triads hide out disguised as nuns.

Cast Includes: Eric Idle, Robbie Coltrane

Once Upon a Time in Little Italy (1999)

A few struggling actors pose as a Mafia family to survive financially in New York.

Cast Includes: Vittorio Gassman

One Thrilling Night (1942)

A small-town newlywed couple spend their wedding night at a New York City hotel and get involved with gangsters.

Cast Includes: John Beal

Oscar (1991)

A mobster who promised to go straight has problems meeting his goal.

Cast Includes: Sylvester Stallone, Chazz Palminteri

Osso Bucco (2007)

Two mobsters and two detectives with warrants for their arrest are trapped in a restaurant during a historic Chicago snowstorm.

Cast Includes: Mike Starr, Illeana Douglas

Pals (1987 TV)

After two residents of a trailer park discover over $3,000,000 in an abandoned car, they get in trouble with the mobster who hid it there.

Cast Includes: Don Ameche, George C. Scott

Perrier's Bounty (2009)

After a loan-shark enforcer is accidentally killed by a debtor's neighbor, a gangster pursues the debtor, the neighbor, and the debtor's father.

Cast Includes: Gabriel Byrne, Jim Broadbent

Pizza with Bullets (2010)

Revived from near-death by the smell of pizza, a mob boss thinks the pizza maker is his long lost-son and the second-in-command thinks both the mob boss and the pizza maker should die.

Cast Includes: Vincent Pastore, Talia Shire

Plan B (2001)

After a bookkeeper thinks she killed three mobsters, her boss makes her a hit woman.

Cast Includes: Paul Sorvino, Diane Keaton

The Plot Against Harry (1989)

When a small-time Jewish mobster gets out of prison, he finds that things have changed dramatically with his neighborhood and family.

Cast Includes: Martin Priest

Police Academy: Mission to Moscow (1994)

The Police Academy crew is hired by the Russian government to help fight the Russian Mafia.

Cast Includes: Ron Perlman, Michael Winslow

The Pope Must Diet (1991)

A priest who is mistakenly named Pope must deal with Vatican corruption and the mob.

Cast Includes: Robbie Coltrane, Alex Rocco

Prizzi's Honor (1985)

After a hit man and a hit woman fall in love, they find out that they've been contracted to kill each other.

Cast Includes: Jack Nicholson, Kathleen Turner, Anjelica Houston

Pronto (1997 TV)

A bookie in trouble with the mob retires to Greece, but mobsters follow his girlfriend to find him.

Cast Includes: Peter Falk

Proper Villains (2011)

The lives of two small-time collectors who work for a bookie get shook up after they accidentally back over a hit man.
Cast Includes: William Orendorff

Rackety Rax (1932)

After a racketeer starts a college to get an advantage in betting on college football games, his rival gets his own college football team.
Cast Includes: Victor McLaglen

A Rage in Harlem (1991)

After a gangster's moll arrives in Harlem with a truck full of stolen gold and her old associates in pursuit, she meets a naïve accountant who relies on his worldlier stepbrother to help them.
Cast Includes: Forest Whitaker, Gregory Hines

Rancid Aluminum (2000)

After inheriting the family firm, a man finds out that it's bankrupt and his only chance to save it is by doing business with the Russian Mafia.
Cast Includes: Joseph Fiennes

Mob Reflexology

Randy and the Mob (2007)
A good old boy gets in trouble with mobsters and receives help from his identical twin brother who is gay.
Cast Includes: Ray McKinnon, Lisa Blount

Revenge of the Pink Panther (1978)
A police inspector believed dead at the hands of French mobsters investigates why he was targeted for death.
Cast Includes: Peter Sellers

Rise And Shine (1941)
A stupid college football player is kidnapped by gangsters who have bet heavily on the other team.
Cast Includes: Jack Oakie, Milton Berle, George Murphy

The Ritz (1976)
A man on the run from the mob hides out in a gay bath house.
Cast Includes: Jack Weston, Rita Moreno, Jerry Stiller, Kay Ballard

Robin and the Seven Hoods (1964)
Two racketeers in prohibition-era Chicago fight for control of the town and one of them gains public support by donating money to an orphanage.
Cast Includes: Frank Sinatra, Dean Martin, Sammy Davis Jr., Bing Crosby

Rush Hour 2 (2001)
A Los Angeles detective and a Hong Kong detective stumble into a money-counterfeiting operation run by an American crime boss and a Triad gang leader.
Cast Includes: Jackie Chan, Chris Tucker

Safe Men (1998)
Two singers mistaken for professional safe crackers run into trouble with gangsters in Rhode Island.
Cast Includes: Sam Rockwell, Paul Giamatti, Mark Ruffalo

See Spot Run (2001)
After a mob boss targets an FBI drug-sniffing dog for death, the dog is put in witness protection but escapes and hides in a mail truck.
Cast Includes: David Arquette, Paul Sorvino, Michael Clarke Duncan

Shark City (2009)
Two friends in New York get involved with the mob when one falls in love with a mob boss' daughter and the other swindles the mob boss out of $1,000,000.
Cast Includes: Vivica A. Fox, Corey Haim

She Had to Eat (1937)

A gas station owner is mistaken for an escaped killer and pursued by police and gangsters.

Cast Includes: Jack Haley, Arthur Treacher

The Shipment (2001)

A New York mobster planning to hijack a truck carrying a shipment of Viagra in Arizona runs into trouble when the truck's driver steals it first.

Cast Includes: Matthew Modine, Elizabeth Berkeley, Robert Loggia

Shoot Em Up (2007)

After a man helps a pregnant woman escape from a gunman and deliver her baby, he protects the child from a gang that wants to kill it.

Cast Includes: Clive Owen, Paul Giamatti

Sister Act (1992)

A Vegas lounge singer who witnesses a mob murder hides in a convent and helps the nuns develop a successful choir.

Cast Includes: Whoopee Goldberg, Maggie Smith, Harvey Keitel

Six Ways to Sunday (1997)

An 18-year-old boy joins the Jewish mob as a hit man to support his mother.

Cast Includes: Deborah Harry, Adrien Brody

Skidoo (1968)

When a mobster refuses to come out of retirement to kill someone, the mob leader kidnaps his daughter.

Cast Includes: Jackie Gleason, Carol Channing, Frankie Avalon, Groucho Marx

Sleepy Lagoon (1943)

A reformist mayor inadvertently allows gangsters to develop a gambling hall beneath an amusement park in a small town.

Cast Includes: Judy Canova, Dennis Day

Smokin' Aces (2006)

Federal agents must protect a magician who has agreed to testify against the Las Vegas mob after a mob boss puts out a large contract on his life.

Cast Includes: Ryan Reynolds, Ray Liotta, Ben Affleck, Jeremy Piven

Smokin' Stogies (2001)

When a million dollars worth of smuggled Cuban cigars disappears in Miami, a New York mob boss sends one of his men to find them.

Cast Includes: Tony Sirico, Frank Vincent, Joseph Marino

Snatch (2000)

A stolen diamond is pursued by amateur boxing promoters, bookies and Russian gangsters, among others.

Cast Includes: Brad Pitt, Benicio Del Toro, Dennis Farina

So You Won't Talk (1940)

After a book reviewer shaves his beard, he looks exactly like a gangster who has just been released from prison, and he is plagued by the gangster's old mob.

Cast Includes: Joe E. Brown

So's Your Aunt Emma (1942)

A middle-aged spinster becomes involved in the fight rackets when gangsters mistake her for Ma Barker while she's visiting the boxer son of her childhood boyfriend.

Cast Includes: Zasu Pitts

Some Like It Hot (1959)

After two male musicians witness the St. Valentine's Day massacre, they escape the mob by disguising themselves as women and joining an all-girl band.

Cast Includes: Marilyn Monroe, Tony Curtis, Jack Lemmon

Spike of Bensonhurst (1988)

A young, aspiring boxer from an Italian section of Brooklyn falls in love with a mob boss' daughter and is forced to move to a Puerto Rican section of Brooklyn.

Cast Includes: Ernest Borgnine

Stark Raving Mad (2002)

A small time hustler throws a rave next to a bank so he can steal a priceless sculpture stored in the bank's vault and pay off his brother's debt to a crime lord.

Cast Includes: Sean William Scott, Lou Diamond Phillips

The Stork Pays Off (1941)

A mobster and his crew take over a rival's nightclub only to learn that it's really a nursery.

Cast Includes: Max "Slapsie Maxie" Rosenbloom

The Sting (1973)

Two con men team up to get revenge on a mob boss who killed their friend.

Cast Includes: Paul Newman, Robert Redford

Strike Me Pink (1936)

A meek man gets involved with mobsters at an amusement park.
Cast Includes: Eddie Cantor, Ethel Mermen

Suicide Kings (1997)

Four friends kidnap an ex-mob boss to collect a ransom to use to pay off other kidnappers who took the sister of one of the friends.

Cast Includes: Christopher Walken, Denis Leary

Sweet Genevieve (1947)

Racketeers move into town and get high school kids interested in gambling and other dubious activities.

Cast Includes: Jean Porter

Swing It Professor (1937)

After being fired for not knowing swing, a music professor moves to Chicago and gets involved with a nightclub and gangsters.

Cast Includes: Milburn Stone

Table One (2000)

When four friends can't repay money borrowed from the mob to open a restaurant, the mob turns the restaurant into a nudie bar.

Cast Includes: Stephen Baldwin

They Call Me Bruce? (1982)

A Korean man who looks like martial arts legend Bruce Lee gets mixed up in mob-related activities.

Cast Includes: Johnny Yune, Marguax Hemmingway

Thieves Fall Out (1941)

A man sells his anticipated inheritance to gangsters who kidnap his grandmother when they can't force his father to buy it back.

Cast Includes: Eddie Albert, Alan Hale, Jane Darwell

Things Change (1988)

After a shoe-shiner resembling a Mafia boss is paid to confess to a murder he didn't commit, he is taken for a last fling in Lake Tahoe by the low-level mobster who is guarding him.

Cast Includes: Don Ameche, Joe Mantegna

Tight Shoes (1941)

After a mobster takes over a shoe store for a gambling operation, a former salesman at the store exposes him to the authorities.

Cast Includes: Broderick Crawford, Shemp Howard

Triggermen (2002)

A Chicago mob boss mistakes two small-time British hoodlums as hit men who are supposed to eliminate his rival, while the real hit men wait for his instructions and debate their options.

Cast Includes: Pete Postlethwaite, Amanda Plummer

The Troublemaker (1964)

A chicken farmer who opens a coffee house in New York's Greenwich Village must deal with the mob and other problems.

Cast Includes: James Frawley, Buck Henry, Godfrey Cambridge

True Identity (1991)
A black actor disguises himself as a white man in order to evade mobsters.
Cast Includes: Lenny Henry, Frank Langella, Peggy Lipton

True Romance (1993)
Alabama newlyweds go to Hollywood with cocaine and gangsters pursue them.
Cast Includes: Christian Slater, Patricia Arquette, Dennis Hopper

Two Hands (1999)
A teenager goes on the run from the mob when some of their money disappears.
Cast Includes: Heath Ledger

Two's a Mob (1998)
A quirky, dysfunctional crime family gets into comic adventures as the head of the family straightens out messes caused by his adopted son.
Cast Includes: Jonathan Koensgen

The Undertaker's Wedding (1997)
An undertaker profiting from a local mob war becomes romantically involved with the wife of the mob boss' brother while the brother gets involved with the undertaker's girlfriend.
Cast Includes: Adrien Brody, Jeff Wincott

Up Your Alley (1942) (aka Bang! Bang! The Mafia Gang)
A catering company employee goes to a Hollywood party and impersonates a Mafia boss.
Cast Includes: Cheri Caffaro

Very Mean Men (2000)
A bartender tells a story of a mob war that began when someone didn't leave a tip for a waitress.
Cast Includes: Matthew Modine, Martin Landau, Ben Gazzara

Warm Blooded Killers (1999)

Brother and sister contract killers who lead an otherwise normal suburban Los Angeles life become involved in jobs that require them to kill an innocent man or suffer the consequences.

Cast Includes: Mick Murray, Constance Zimmer

Watch Out, We're Mad (1974)

Two stunt car drivers want revenge when the mob destroys a dune buggy they were trying to win.

Cast Includes: Donald Pleasence

We're in the Legion Now (1936)

Two mobsters join the French Foreign Legion in order to get away from their enemies.

Cast Includes: Reginald Denny

Who Do I Gotta Kill? (1994)

A writer suffering from writer's block takes a job with the mob in order to support himself.

Cast Includes: Vincent Pastore, Sandra Bullock

Whole Lotta Sole (2011)

A man in debt to a mobster tries to rob a fish market owned by the mobster and then holes up in a local store after taking a bunch of oddball hostages.

Cast Includes: Kevin Bacon

The Whole Nine Yards (2000)

A hit man wanted by the Chicago mob moves next door to a Montreal dentist whose wife gets him to go to Chicago, rat him out and claim a finder's fee while she tries to get the hit man to kill her husband.

Cast Includes: Bruce Willis, Matthew Perry, Rosanna Arquette

The Whole Ten Yards (2004)

A retired hit man helps his dentist neighbor recover his wife who has been kidnapped by the Hungarian mob. Sequel to *The Whole Nine Yards*.

Cast Includes: Bruce Willis, Matthew Perry, Amanda Peet

Wise Guys (1986)

Two errand boys for the mob are set up to kill each other after they lose a lot of money.

Cast Includes: Danny DeVito, Joe Piscopo, Harvey Keitel, Patti LuPone

Whistling in the Dark (1933)

After a mystery writer devises a plan for the perfect murder, a gangster who learns of it decides to use it.

Cast Includes: Edward Arnold, Nat Pendleton

Wonder Man (1945)

A nightclub entertainer murdered by a gangster comes back as a ghost and enlists his meek twin brother to help avenge his death.

Cast Includes: Danny Kaye, Virginia Mayo

The Wrong Arm of the Law (1963)

Police and gangsters in London team up to defeat a gang that poses as police and steals from gangsters.

Cast Includes: Peter Sellars

You Kill Me (2007)

An alcoholic hit man from Buffalo is sent to San Francisco to do an AA program, meets a quirky woman, and returns to Buffalo to take care of mob business.

Cast Includes: Ben Kingsley, Tea Leoni, Luke Wilson, Dennis Farina

CHAPTER EIGHT
Mob Movie Quotes

Film fans know that the most memorable mob movie quotes—the ones that become a permanent part of our popular culture—come from serious mob movies. There's Marlon Brando's "I coulda been a contender" in *On The Waterfront*. There's Al Pacino's "Say hello to my Little Friend" in *Scarface*. In *GoodFellas* there's Joe Pesci's: "But, I'm funny how? Funny like a clown? I amuse you? I make you laugh?" And of course, there's the most famous line of all: "I'm going to make him an offer he can't refuse" from *The Godfather*.

Quotes from mob comedies aren't as memorable. But they are funnier. Here are a few examples.

The Adventures of Pluto Nash

Dina Lake: What makes you so sure he'll help us out?

Pluto Nash: Oh, he'll help us. He couldn't sing a note if it weren't for me.

Dina Lake: You taught Tony Francis how to sing?

Pluto Nash: No, I convinced a bookie not to pour some acid down his throat.

Pluto Nash: You married twins?

Tony Francis: No, I met the perfect woman, so I had her cloned.

Dina Lake: Which one is which?

Tony Francis: Who cares?

Analyze That

Dr. Ben Sobel: Lou the Wrench? Why the Wrench?

Paul Vitti: He twisted some guy's head off.

Dr. Ben Sobel: OFF?

Dr. Ben Sobel: I thought you were in prison?

Jelly: It would appear not.

Dr. Ben Sobel: How'd you get out?

Jelly: I had a new trial. Turns out that the evidence in the first trial was tainted.

Dr. Ben Sobel: Oh, I see.

Jelly: Anyway, two of the witnesses decided not to testify and the third guy, well, he committed suicide.

Dr. Ben Sobel: How?

Jelly: He stabbed himself in the back four times and threw himself off a bridge.

Analyze This

Dr. Sobel: You don't hear the word "No" very often, do you?

Paul Vitti: I hear it all the time, only it's more like "No! Please! No! No!"

Be Cool

Elliot Wilhelm: When are you going to call me?

Chili Palmer: When your phone rings.

Fast Freddie: Who are all these people trying to kill you?

Chili Palmer: I don't know. I'm in the music business now. It could be anybody.

The Big Hit

Melvin Smiley: Technically, you can call me a hit man.

Keiko Nishi: Really? A hit man? Does that pay well?

Melvin Smiley: Oh, of course. I make a killing.

Broadway Danny Rose

Danny Rose: My rabbi, Rabbi Perlstein, used to say we're all guilty in the eyes of God.

Tina Vitale: Do you believe in God?

Danny Rose: No, no. But I'm guilty over it.

Buddy Buddy

Clooney: Have you ever been married, Mr. Trabucco?

Trabucco: Once but I got rid of her. Now I just lease.

The Crew

Pepper Lowenstein: You torched my house?

Mike "The Brick" Donatelli: We had to make it look like an accident.

Pepper Lowenstein: Oh my God! That house was going to be featured in *Better Home & Gardens*.

Bobby Bartellemeo: Well, you can still be in *Gardens*.

Gigli

Starkman: Louis, you wanna go to medical school?

Louis: Medical school?

[Starkman shoots him]

Starkman: Yeah! Students there can always use something to learn on!

Harlem Nights

Quick: Last ass whoopin' I got was... what, 27 years ago?

Sugar Ray: Yeah, when the doctor slapped your ass.

Quick: Yeah, and I'm still lookin' for him!

Heist

Joe Moore: She could talk her way out of a sunburn.

In Bruges

Chloë: So what do you do, Raymond?

Ray: I... shoot people for money.

Chloë: [smiling] What kinds of people?

Ray: Priests, children... you know, the usual.

Chloë: Is there a lot of money to be made in that business?

Ray: There is for priests. There isn't for children. So what is it you do, Chloë?

Chloë: I sell cocaine and heroin to Belgian film crews.

Ray: Do you?

Chloë: Do I look like I do?

Ray: You do, actually. Do I... look like I shoot people?

Chloë: No. Just children.

Jane Austen's Mafia

Anthony Cortino: You lost a lot of blood but we found most of it.

Anthony Cortino: Gianini... any Sicilian in you?

Pepper Gianini: Not since last night.

Johnny Dangerously

Dutch: You can't park here. This is a handicapped zone.

Danny Vermin: I am handicapped. I'm psychotic.

Johnny: Say kid, what do they call you?

Lil: Impressive.

Knockaround Guys

Teddy Deserve: We're gunna get one of the three R's: the roof, the river, or the revolver.

The Last Shot

Joe Devine: Have you actually seen a person die, watched them bleed to death, seen them take their last breath? I've seen that... many times.

Steven Schats: Why have you seen that?

Joe Devine: I used to produce music videos.

The Lemon Drop Kid

Sidney Melbourne: Santy Claus don't drink.

Gloomy Willie: Oh, no? Well, how come he's always falling down chimneys?

Mad Dog Time

Vic: Ben, go home. Pack your bags, and leave town.

Ben London: Nobody tells Ben London what to do any more!

Vic: [shoots Ben in the leg] Ben, hop home, pack your bags, and leave town.

Ben London: I'll hop home whenever I fucking feel like it!

Vic: [shoots the other leg] Now, Ben, roll home, pack your bags, and leave town.

Married To The Mob

Mike Downey: You know, Angela, I've been thinking.

Angela de Marco: Well, there you go, working without tools again.

Angela de Marco: Everything we own fell off a truck!

The Matador

Julian Noble: I'm as serious as an erection problem.

Mobsters and Mormons

Carmine "The Beans" Pasquale: It's rap music these days. Have you heard the names? Puff Daddy...

Vincent Pasquale: He changed it to P. Diddy for short.

Carmine "The Beans" Pasquale: Oh, yeah, like it takes all day to say "Puff".

Bada Bing Club

My Blue Heaven

Vincent "Vinnie" Antonelli: When did your wife leave?

Barney: October.

Vince: That's when my wife left! What is it about the month of October?

Barney: I dunno. The pressure of Halloween? You never know what to go as!

Nuns on the Run

Brian Hope: Look Charlie, some con men sell life insurance. The church sells afterlife insurance. It's brilliant! Everyone thinks you might need it, and no one can prove you don't.

Charlie McManus: The church isn't selling anything, Brian.

Brian Hope: Oh! Well, if the church isn't selling anything, how did it get to be so rich? Just remember, wherever there's a deep human need there's money to be made.

Charlie McManus: You think so?

Brian Hope: Of course; look at Kentucky Fried Chicken.

Charlie McManus: [teaching Brian how to cross himself] Spectacles, testicles, wallet and watch.

Sister Superior: You stole money because you want to get *out* of organized crime?

Brian Hope: Oh, it was stolen already.

Charlie McManus: The important thing is that now the good guys have got it instead of the bad guys.

Brian Hope: Yeah. It's like Robin Hood, you see? We stole from the rich to give to the poor.

Sister Superior: Who are you going to give this money to?

Brian Hope: Us. We're poor.

Brian Hope/Sister Euphemia: Does the Trinity make any sense to you?

Charlie McManus: Oh, no. No, it makes no sense to anyone. That's why you have to believe it. That's why you have to have faith. If it made sense, it wouldn't have to be a religion, would it?

Sister Superior: What happened to your arm?

Faith: I'm not sure. I fell.

Sister Superior: It looks like a bullet wound to me.

Faith: How would you know?

Sister Superior: I've seen bullet wounds. I've been a missionary.

Faith: Where?

Sister Superior: East L. A.

Prizzi's Honor

Irene Walker: Charley, I've been doin' three to four hits a year for the past couple of years, most at full pay.

Charley Partanna: That many?

Irene Walker: Well, it's not many when you consider the size of the population.

Robin and the Seven Hoods

Robbo: You look like the day they fixed the electricity at the death house.

Rush Hour 2

Lee: These men are Triads. The most deadly gang in China.

James Carter: You think they scare me? I'm from Los Angeles, man. We invented gangs!

Shoot Em Up

Mr. Hertz: Bravo, Mr. Hero. Bravo.

Mr. Smith: Why are you trying to kill this woman? [Hertz laughs]

Mr. Smith: Something funny?

Mr. Hertz: Well, I was just remembering a limerick. "There once was a woman who was quite begat. She had three babies named Nat, Pat, and Tat. She said it was fun in the breeding, but found it was hell in the feeding, when she saw there was no tit for Tat." You have caused me no end of trouble, but now I shall return the favor. Tit for tat, right?

Some Like It Hot

Sugar: Real diamonds! They must be worth their weight in gold!

Sugar: Water polo? Isn't that terribly dangerous?
Junior: I'll say. I had two ponies drowned under me.

Suicide Kings

Marty: Don't go dying on me. Remember, I'm a lawyer. I've got friends in hell.

They Call Me Bruce?

Bruce: I am a sex object. I always ask women for sex, and they object.

The Whole Nine Yards

Jill St. Claire: I'm still a virgin. I mean I haven't killed anyone yet.

Wise Guys

Frank "The Fixer" Acavano: Let me waste em, Mr. Costelo!

Anthony Costelo: Do we really hurt them by killing them?

Louie Fontucci: It's a good start.

The Sopranos

While not technically a movie, *The Sopranos* was filmed like one – with a big budget and lots of on-location scenes. The story of a mob family in New Jersey, many fans consider it to be the best television show ever created. *The Sopranos* ran from 1999 through 2007 on HBO where it was the most successful show in the history of the channel. While often depicting the brutality of the mob lifestyle, the show was also laced with humor. Here are some memorable lines of dialogue.

Dr. Jennifer Melfi: When's the last time you had a prostate exam?

Tony Soprano: Hey, I don't even let anybody wag their finger in my face.

Tony Soprano: So, your father tells me you're takin' up uh… astronomy in college.

Kevin Bonpensiero: No. Business.

Tony Soprano: Well, how come he keeps sayin' you're takin' up space in school?

Raymond Curto: You heard about Jimmy Altieri; right?

Big Pussy Bonpensiero: Yeah, flipped… fuckin' asshole.

Paulie Walnuts: He had two assholes when they buried 'im.

Tony Soprano: What is that?

Irina Peltsin: "Chicken Soup for the Soul."

Tony Soprano: You should read "Tomato Sauce for your Ass;" it's the Italian version.

Silvio Dante: She's so fat, her blood type is Ragu.

Paulie Walnuts: Ginny Sacramoni, what she needs is her own zip code.

Paulie Walnuts: She's so fat, when she goes campin', the bears have to hide their food.

Furio Giunta: I like a woman you can grab onto something.

Paulie Walnuts: You grab onto Ginny Sacrimoni, your hands'll disappear.

Gigi Cestone: Jersey's a small state, she moves in... she could tip it over.

Tony Soprano: All right, obviously you told the cops you don't know who did this.

Vito Spatafore: I'm upset. But please, I know how to keep my mouth shut.

Ralph Cifaretto: Oh, unless of course there's a salami sandwich around.

Bobby Baccilieri: One time we went huntin'. Saw a sign that said, "Bear Left." (pause) So we went home.

Bobby Baccilieri: World really went downhill after the World Trade Center. You know, Quasimodo predicted all of this.

Tony Soprano: Who did what?

Bobby Baccilieri: All these problems. The Middle East. The end o' the world.

Tony Soprano: Nostradamus. Quasimodo's the hunchback of Notre Dame.

Bobby Baccilieri: Oh, right. Notredamus.

Tony Soprano: Nostradamus and Notre Dame, that's two different things completely.

Bobby Baccilieri: It's interesting though they'd be so similar, isn't it? And I always thought, "OK, Hunchback of Notre Dame. You also got your quarterback and your halfback of Notre Dame".

Tony Soprano: One's a fucking cathedral!

Bobby Baccilieri: Obviously, I know. I'm just sayin'. It's interesting, the coincidence. What, you're gonna tell me you never pondered that? The back thing with Notre Dame?

Tony Soprano: No!

Paulie Walnuts: You're late.

Ralph Cifaretto: Well, tomorrow I could be on time, but you'll be stupid forever.

Carmela Soprano: You bought a racehorse?

Tony Soprano: No, I didn't buy it.

Carmela Soprano: It followed you home?

Silvio Dante: He was a good kid, Raymond.

Tony Soprano: The best.

Paulie Walnuts: At least he went fast. Not like Dick Barone, poor fuck.

Bobby Baccilieri: Dick Barone died?

Silvio Dante: Lou Gehrig's disease.

Christopher Moltisanti: You ever think what a coincidence it is that Lou Gehrig died of Lou Gehrig's disease?

Tony Soprano: So how was Florida?

Phil Leotardo: Hot and sticky... like my balls.

CHAPTER NINE

A Mob Menagerie:
Rats, Canaries and Stool Pigeons

There's an old saying that speech is silver and silence is golden. Mobsters agree with the silence is golden part, but they don't view speech as silver. To them, speech is cement. Because if you talk, you'll end up in cement boots. It gives a whole new meaning to putting your foot in your mouth. Actually, you don't have to worry about putting your foot in your mouth. If you even open it, they'll put *their* foot in your mouth.

The tradition of "not talking" goes way back with mobsters in every society around the globe. It's the prime directive. No matter what happens keep your mouth shut. That's why people who disobey this rule are referred to with such derision. Squealers. Traitors. Informers. Rats. Stool pigeons. Canaries. It's also why the witness protection program exists.

There's another old saying in the world of mobsters: three people can keep a secret if two of them are dead. That's especially true if two of them are rats or stoolies. In this chapter you'll find humor related to informers and traitors. But you better not tell anyone about it. Capiche?

Witness protection wants to move us to another island.

Stool Pigeons, Rats, and Informers

Q: What do stool pigeons and Slinkies have in common?
A: Neither of them is good for much, but it will make you laugh like hell to watch one roll down a flight of stairs.

Q: What's the difference between a rat and a trampoline?
A: Mobsters take their shoes off to jump on a trampoline.

Q: What's the difference between a football and a stool pigeon?
A: The football goes farther when you kick it.

Q: What's the difference between a car full of informers and a porcupine?
A: With a porcupine, the pricks are on the outside!

Q: What does it mean when a rat is gasping for breath?
A: You didn't hold the pillow down long enough.

Q: How do you save a stool pigeon from drowning?
A: Take your foot off his head.

Q: What did the mobster's son tell his dad when he failed his examination?
A: Dad, they questioned me for 3 hours, but I never told them anything.

Q: How does a gorilla become another animal?
A: When a Mafia don hires a big gorilla to be his bodyguard and the big ape goes to the cops and turns into a stool pigeon!

Q: What do you have when an informer is buried up to his neck in wet cement?
A: Not enough cement.

Q: What's the difference between onions and rats?
A: I cry when I cut up onions.

Q: What is the difference between a stool pigeon and a baby?
A: The baby will stop whining after awhile.

Q: What do informers in the witness protection program and hemorrhoids have in common?
A: They're both a pain in the butt and never seem to go completely away.

Q: What do you do if you run over a rat?
A: Reverse.

Q: What do you call a stool pigeon with no arms, legs or tongue?
A: Trustworthy.

Q: Why do all informers run fast?
A: Because the slow ones are dead or in witness protection.

Q: What's the difference between Elvis and a drowned stool pigeon?
A: Elvis was bloated BEFORE he died.

Q: When do you smile at an informer?
A: When you read his obituary.

Q: What's the difference between an informer with a pink neck and a purple neck?
A: A hit man's grip around it.

Q: Why do people take an instant dislike to stool pigeons?
A: It saves time.

Q: What is the difference between an informer and a skunk?
A: Nobody wants to hit a skunk.

Q: What do rats miss most about a great mob party?
A: The invitation.

Stoolie Knock-Knock Joke

Knock Knock

Who's there?

I'm in the car trunk.

Headline Hits: Rats and Canaries

Canary Nearly Blew The Tweet Life
(*New York Post*, June 18, 2001)

"Mob stoolie William Marshall is expected to testify in the Gold Club trial in Atlanta this week, and will explain how he was released from prison, got paid $75,000, and was moved to a safehouse in Vermont for cooperating with the feds against John A. 'Junior' Gotti in 1998.

"But the muscle-bound mobster wannabe will also be asked to explain how he nearly blew his deal by paging and making collect calls to old cronies from his secret hideaway, according to Marshall's grand jury testimony and FBI reports obtained by *The Post*."

Mob Canary Is a Chicken!
'Balks' in Don Trial
(*New York Post*, September 15, 2006)

"A Brooklyn mobster who made himself a Miami club king and then saved himself years in prison by ratting out his cohorts has finally decided there's one man in the Mafia he will not cross.

"Chris Paciello—who palled around with the likes of Madonna and Nikki Taylor during his salad days in the 1990s—is now 'balking' at testifying against acting Colombo crime-family boss Alphonse 'Allie Boy' Persico, according to a new report."

Mob Canary to Warble Hit Song Today

(New York Post, April 26, 2004)

"It's payback time for a wiseguy who took two bullets in a failed Colombo mob hit.

"Joseph Campanella, 45, is set to make his debut as a witness for the feds today as the trial of two alleged hit men, reputed mobster Vincent 'Chicky' DeMartino and associate Giovanni 'John the Barber' Floridia, gets under way in Brooklyn federal court."

Rat Pack's Set to Squeal
Canaries to Sing Gambinos' Greatest Hits

(New York Post, February 12, 2008)

"The dirty-dozen mob informants threatening to bring down the Gambino crime family include would-be victims who narrowly escaped rubouts—and some of the hit men who tried to kill them."

Mob Rat Makes Wise Quacks at Trial

(Daily News, New York, January 15, 2004)

"Shooting stool pigeons is time-honored mob sport. But shooting ducks?

"At least for a moment yesterday, that's what former Luchese crime family boss Alphonse (Little Al) D'Arco apparently hoped a jury would believe.

"Testifying at the murder-racketeering trial of mobster Louis (Louie Crossbay) Daidone, D'Arco, a key government witness, acknowledged under cross-examination he kept all sorts of guns in his wife's Florida condo.

"'Let's talk about the sawed-off shotguns you kept there,' pressed defense lawyer Anthony Lombardino. 'They're used for one thing, to murder.'

"'They're used for other things,' insisted D'Arco. 'To go duck hunting.'

"'You use sawed-off shotguns to go duck hunting?' an incredulous Lombardino shot back.

"D'Arco backed down and Lombardino went on, 'What about the machine guns?' he asked. 'That's also used to hunt ducks?'"

Witness Protection

I'm in the Jehovah Witness' Protection program. I have to go door to door and tell people I'm someone else.
– Steven Wright

My uncle testified at the trial of an organized crime boss and then begged to be put into the witness-protection program. Instead, the FBI got him a job as a sales clerk at Kmart. It's been six months and no one's been able to find him.
– Jay Trachman

There's a rumor that NBC is so upset with me, they want to keep me off the air for three years. That's what they say. Yeah, my response to that is, if NBC doesn't want people to see me, just leave me on NBC. It's like I'll be in the witness protection program.
– Conan O'Brien

I've always wanted to be in the witness protection program. Fresh start. No debts, no baggage. Already got my name picked out. Lord Rupert Everton. I am a shipping merchant who raises fancy dogs. That's the life.
– Steve Carell as Michael Scott

The Phone Call

An old retired mob boss lived alone in Brooklyn. He wanted to plant a vegetable garden in his backyard, but he was getting too old for that kind of physical labor. So he called his son, also a mobster. He said, "I want to dig up the whole backyard to plant a vegetable garden. So send some of your crew over with shovels." The son said, "Whaddaya kidding me? Don't dig up ANYTHING!!! Did you forget all the bodies we buried there? Just wait till I come over." The police had tapped the phone line and heard the whole thing. They raced to the old man's home, dug up the whole yard and didn't find a single body. They apologized and left. Ten minutes later the old mobster's phone rang. His son said, "Now that they dug up the garden, we'll be over tomorrow to plant it."

CHAPTER TEN
You Can't Make This Stuff Up

Sometimes truth is stranger than fiction—especially with the mob. In this chapter you'll find lots of examples.

Cursive Writing

On December 21, 2007, the *Daily News* in New York reported that a federal judge unsealed a handwritten incantation that Vincent "Vinny Gorgeous" Bascino stashed in his shoe during his 2006 trial for racketeering. The spell, designed to put a curse on prosecutors, FBI agents and mob turncoats, goes: "Before the house of the judge, three dead men look out the window, one having no tongue, the other no lungs, and the third was sick, blind and dumb." It was apparently ineffective. Basciano was convicted of murder and racketeering.

Next time he should use a more powerful curse: Roses are red. Your face is blue. You're gonna be dead if I don't stop choking you.

Green Thumbs Up

On July 20, 2006, the *Daily News* (New York) reported that John "Johnny Goggles" Baudanza, an alleged Mafioso awaiting trial for racketeering, asked a judge to modify his bail agreement so he can work at his "design and landscape business." He has been under house arrest since posting bail of $2 million. His lawyer argues that Baudanza's business will fail without him and that he's just trying to support his wife and kids. The article notes that the feds claim Baudanza, who has a reputation for violence, is "more an expert in hurt-i-culture than horticulture" and that the business is just a front.

Even if the landscape business is just a front, you know he's got to be great at weed whacking.

In Translation

On July 16, 2007, the *Chicago Sun Times* reported that a wise guy, testifying against his mobster father, told jurors the meaning of "mobspeak" terms used by his father during secretly recorded conversations. For example, collecting a "recipe" referred to shaking down a victim for protection money. A "dry beef" was a stool pigeon who talked with the FBI but wouldn't testify. And a mobster who never killed anyone was someone who "never moved one stone in his life." Unfortunately, the code worked so well that the mobster was sometimes unintelligible as shown by this exchange: "Don't send nobody to see the sister that's sick," Calabrese Sr. told his son in one conversation. "Don't have nobody see her. Just leave it go till. . ." "I'm lost," his son confessed.

Just take care of that thing or I'll take care of you, if you know what I mean.

What's Cooking?

On September 5, 2003, United Press International reported that Montreal Mafia boss Frank Cotroni, who had recently been released from prison, received permission from his parole officer to pursue plans for publishing a cookbook.

His favorite recipe is breakfast in bed with horse's head.

A Song in My Heart and a Gun in My Hand

On April 17, 2009, UPI reported that legendary mobster Al Capone had composed a love song that would be released on the Internet. Called "Madonna Mia," the song was composed while Capone resided in Alcatraz in the 1930s. It has been described as "a very touching Italian love ballad."

An earlier version was written as a dance tune called "I'm On The Rock Around The Clock."

Translating Help Wanted Ads

On November 27, 2003, the *Courier Mail* in Brisbane, Australia reported that a large Yakuza gang was advertising for new recruits in Japanese sports newspapers. The ads promised meals, lodging and high pay for "bodyguards" and "chauffeurs". Police learned about the recruitment drive from an applicant who called the phone number in the ad. He was dismayed to learn he'd have to go to a Yakuza office for an interview "for joining the Yakuza syndicate."

Hey, the ad was for a chauffeur. Didn't he think he'd have to "take someone for a ride?"

Oops

On October 24, 2008, *The Telegraph* in London reported that a small-time Mafia gang in Italy sent a donkey's head to a shopkeeper who wouldn't pay protection money. The threat was apparently inspired by the "The Godfather" film in which mobsters place a horse's head in the bed of an uncooperative Hollywood producer. But in the film, the head comes from one of the producer's prize stallions. The donkey's head had no similar meaning. And the shopkeeper was so confused he thought it was a practical joke. The gang that sent the donkey's head have been called "idiots."

Now that's what's called making an ass of yourself.

Book Him

On June 22, 2009, the *New York Post* reported that reformed mob boss Michael Franzese has written a book of business advice based on his experience running an organized crime operation. Entitled *I'll Make You an Offer You Can't Refuse: Insider Business Tips From a Former Mob Boss*, the book argues that rules for success in the Mafia also apply to the Fortune 500.

Advice includes how to really cement relationships, shoot to the top, and give golden parachutes that don't open.

Next the Easter Bunny

On December 21, 2008, the *Daily Star* (United Kingdom) reported that Italian police uncovered a Mafia plan to steal relics from the tomb of St. Nicholas—better known to the world as Santa Claus. Authorities believe the mob has moved into the black market trade for relics and antiques due to the world financial crisis.

A spokesman for the Mafia denied the allegations and claimed the relics "fell off the back of the sleigh."

They're Back

On March 6, 2010, the *Daily News* in New York reported that a new reality TV show, "Ghostfellas," would involve making contact with the spirits of mob victims. The star of the show is a detective who claims "intuitive" powers. Relatives of people whacked by the mob will accompany him to areas where ghosts of their deceased loved ones are likely to gather. The pilot for the show was shot in a Staten Island wildlife refuge known as a mob dumping ground.

The second show will feature a travelogue of New Jersey.

Next Time Get Magazines From Your Doctor's Office

On January 24, 2008, LawFuel Legal News Service reported that a Gambino crime family member and several associates were charged with operating a magazine subscription telemarketing company in Florida that made fraudulent sales to victims throughout the country. The indictment included charges of mail fraud, wire fraud, money laundering and false statements to the FBI.

The magazines they were selling should have provided a clue: Boys' Life Sentence; O, The Omerta Magazine; Readers' Diegest; and It's Just Business Week.

Sign of the Times

On January 20, 2009, *The Guardian* (United Kingdom) reported that Yakuza mobsters were receiving millions of dollars of welfare in Japan. But it's not all fraud. Mobsters who have been kicked out of the Yakuza are legitimately allowed to collect welfare. Active Yakuza members are not. Tougher laws on prostitution and loan sharking combined with a global recession have made times tough for many Japanese mobsters. And many are going on the dole.

Many now hold signs on street corners, "Will Break Bones For Food."

It's the Law

On September 7, 2009 the *Guardian* (United Kingdom) reported that thousands of members of Japan's largest Yakuza gang were now required to take a 12-page exam to ensure they understood all the details of an anti-organized crime law. They were ordered to do so by their gang leaders. Why? The law allows Yakuza dons to be sued for crimes committed by their underlings. And the dons don't want court fines cutting into their profits. By giving the exam, bosses make sure their troops know the law's prohibitions and the loopholes to get around them. For example, one briefing distributed by a Yakuza group advises "It is now illegal to give financial rewards or promote someone who was involved in a hit against a member of a rival gang. But it is not illegal to give them a salary with a front company and promote them within that organization."

Is it illegal to cheat on the exam?

Bite Worse than Bark

On December 25, 2007, the *Daily News* of New York reported that the wife of mob boss John Gotti Jr. was bitten on the arm by the family's pit bull puppy. A source said that the dog didn't seem to have a vicious bone in his body. The family denied rumors that they had the dog whacked.

It just took a long walk off a short pier.

It's in the Bag

On February 21, 2002, the *Courier Mail* in Brisbane, Australia reported that Yakuza gangsters were receiving special treatment from Japanese post offices. A government survey revealed that bags of Yakuza mail were marked with a special seal that ensured prompt delivery.

Or else.

Have I Got a Deal for You

On November 18, 2010, the Agence France-Presse reported that an anti-Mafia leader in Italy whose business was ruined by gangsters put his organs and body parts up for sale. He hopes to raise enough money to keep his business from going under. Gangsters destroyed his property and scared away clients after he stopped paying protection money. In order to avoid bankruptcy, he's selling his organs to the highest bidder. He said, "I'm open to offers from anyone who wants a kidney, a bit of my liver, a leg." In addition to saving his business, he noted that he's trying to keep a roof over his head.

Unless he sells his head too.

Job Creation

On May 3, 1999, *The Palm Beach Post* in Florida reported that mobsters in Taiwan were paying college tuition for needy students who agree to work for the mob after graduation. The mob needs them as accountants, lawyers and other professionals.

Otherwise they'd have to get student loans and pay the vig.

Really Hot Goods

On September 16, 2009, *The Guardian* (United Kingdom) reported that a submerged ship off the Italian coast might have been sunk by the Mafia to dispose of radioactive waste. The position of the ship matched an account given to authorities by a mob boss. He said his clan got almost $200,000 for dumping the nuclear waste that came from Norway.

They couldn't get anyone to fence it.

Not Guilty

On February 18, 2003, Ananova reported that medical experts at the University of Palermo in Sicily have found that real life godfathers are now seeking psychiatric help. "They come to discuss food disorders, anxiety, depression and sexual problems they are having," said psychiatrist Girolamo Lo Verso. His research shows that Mafioso are trying to deal with the stress caused by their work. One of his more interesting findings: "These men of honor as they like to call themselves have no feelings of guilt no matter how many people they may have killed."

Obviously, they didn't examine any Jewish mobsters.

The Rules

On May 9, 2007, Reuters reported that Italian police found a list of "10 commandments" for mobsters in the home of Salvatore Lo Piccolo, the Sicilian Mafia's top boss. These included:

1. Don't look at friends' wives.

2. Don't visit bars.

3. Don't steal from Mafia families.

4. Respect appointments.

5. Treat wives with respect.

6. Never be godfather to a police officer's children.

7. Always be available for Cosa Nostra even if your wife is about to give birth.

8. Don't behave badly and must hold moral values.

Some rules they forgot include: Always keep your brass knuckles polished; wash your hands before beating; and respect victims by vacuuming the carpet before you roll them up in it.

ET Don't Phone Home

On November 25, 2008, *The Daily Mail* in London reported that Italian police raided a Mafia gang and discovered a device that looked like a mobile phone but was actually a gun. Holding four bullets, the phone is fired by touching a particular key on the keypad. The gun's barrel is disguised as the phone's antenna.

It's called a "Don't Get Smart" phone.

Don't Have a Cow

On October 25, 2006, *Biology* reported that a South Korean scientist attempting to clone dinosaurs purchased what he thought was mammoth remains from the Russian Mafia. He's on trial for misappropriation of public funds. On official claim forms, he expensed money to the Russians as "money for cows."

The Russian mob milked him for a lot of moo-la.

I Shoot Therefore I Am

On June 16, 2007, *The Guardian* (United Kingdom) reported that when Italian police found the bullet-riddled body of a Mafia leader, they discovered he'd been taking a university philosophy exam the day before his demise. His professor at Palermo University said the mobster would have done very well. He had enrolled in the philosophy course while in prison and began classes after his release.

He proved his own ex-istence.

Just Kidding

On September 19, 2006, the *Daily News* in New York reported that prosecutors, arguing that defendant John Gotti Jr. never left the Mafia, presented the jury with a list of "Top 20 Reasons Gotti Never Withdrew." These included: Gotti passed messages to mob pals from prison, and Gotti received rent from properties purchased with mob money. The article noted the similarity to a David Letterman Top 10 list and suggested these additional reasons:

10. Velour sweat suits still in the closet.
9. Stash of frozen horse heads in the garage.
8. Friends who go by nicknames like Johnny Boy, Tommy Sneakers and Jackie Nose...

Gotti's lawyers countered the David Letterman argument with the Rodney Dangerfield defense: "John Gotti Jr. gets no respect. He makes offers you CAN refuse."

Reality TV

On December 18, 2004, Reuters reported that Michele Catalano, a Mafioso in Sicily, was arrested while watching television. Italian police burst into his room to find him watching "The Boss of Bosses," a mini-series about the arrest of real-life Cosa Nostra leader Salvatore "Toto" Riina. Catalano is alleged to be a senior commander for the latest "boss of bosses," Salvatore Lo Piccolo, who succeeded Riina years ago.

He should have been watching "Let's Make A Deal."

CHAPTER ELEVEN
Nick Names and Other Word Play

On February 6, 2008, in the United States District Court of the Eastern District of New York, the United States of America filed an indictment against 62 alleged mobsters. The names, as they appeared on the indictment, included:

Thomas Cacciapoli, also known as "Tommy Sneakers"

Joseph Casiere, also known as "Joe Rackets"

John D'Amico, also known as "Jackie the Nose"

Nicholas Corozzo, also known as "Little Nicky"

Leonard Dimaria, also known as "The Conductor"

Anthony Licata, also known as "Cheeks"

Michael Urciuoli, also known as "Mike the Electrician"

I have a feeling we don't want to know how "Mike the Electrician" got his nickname.

Nicknames have long played a colorful role in the history of the American underworld. It seems like successful mobsters all have a gun, a gang and a nickname. And they're not limited to Italian mobsters. Jewish mobsters have included Abe "Kid Twist" Reles, Benjamin "Bugsy" Siegel, Arnold "The Brain" Rothstein and Israel "Icepick Willie" Alderman. (Can you guess how Icepick got his nickname?) In fact, Otto "Abbadabba" Berman is credited with coining the phrase "Nothing personal; it's just business."

South of the border, the Mafia in Mexico also has its share of interesting nicknames. On July 18, 2004, the *Los Angeles Times* ran an article about a gang charged with murder and kidnapping by Mexico City police. Who was in the gang? According to the *Times*:

> There was "El Salivotas" (the Drooler), "El Guero" (Blondie), "El Enano" (the Dwarf), "El Duende" (the Elf), "El Cejas," (Eyebrows), and "El Tamalon" (the Big Tamale).

With names like those they'd fit right into the American crime scene.

Unsurprisingly, the media has a field day playing with mobster nicknames in headlines and articles. The puns are relentless. If puns were bullets, newspaper readers might die in a hail of hilarity. Of course, humorous wordplay about organized crime goes far beyond nicknames. Definitions, slang terminology and even poetry can come into play. In this chapter, you'll find all sorts of wordplay inspired by mob activity.

Hey Boss, I'm on YousTube!

Headline Hits:
Nicknames Make the News

Stoolies Put Bite on Mobster Bagels

(*Daily News*, New York, January 24, 2004)

"Louie Bagels got creamed.

"Acting Luchese mob boss Louis (Louie Bagels) Daidone was convicted yesterday of racketeering and murder, laid low by five Mafia turncoats."

Drop Dead, Gorgeous
Ma to Killer: Burn in Hell

(*Daily News*, New York, April 1, 2008)

"The mother of a gangland slay victim cursed Bonanno big Vincent 'Vinny Gorgeous' Basciano to hell as he was given a life sentence yesterday for the murder.

"I'm sure you know who Lucifer is," sneered Grace Santoro, 77, whose son, Frank, was shot dead by Basciano and his henchmen on Feb. 14, 2001, as Santoro walked his dog in The Bronx."

Picky, Picky! 'Nose' Is Gross

(*New York Post*, July 15, 2010)

"Say it's snot so.

"A reputed crime-family captain, with the nom-de-mob 'Big Nose,' dug in for some nasal gabagool during an appearance in Brooklyn federal court yesterday—picking and pulling the entire time the judge instructed the jury on deliberations.

"Then he disgustingly licked every finger.

"Anthony Antico, 74, who is on trial on for a variety of racketeering charges, spent a good 10 minutes probing his proboscis."

Mob 'Haha' a Canned Laugh Now

(*New York Post*, January 8, 2005)

"Reputed mobster Louis 'Louie HaHa' Attanasio didn't have much to laugh at yesterday when a federal judge ordered him held behind bars after a year on the lam in the sunny Caribbean."

Can't Keep Nose Clean

(*New York Post*, February 12, 2009)

"Just when he thought he was out . . .

"Jailed crime boss Jackie 'The Nose' D'Amico—who finishes a two-year stint for extortion this November—was charged by the feds yesterday with arranging a 1989 hit on a Staten Island man believed by mobsters to be a government informant."

Mafia 'Tomato' Gets Squished
Raids on SI Bet Ring Bear Fruit

(*New York Post*, November 19, 2009)

"Cops plucked the 'Top Tomato' of a Staten Island sports-betting operation yesterday, along with a rogues' gallery of leg breakers, bookies and corrupt government workers involved in two resurgent Mafia factions, authorities said.

"The early-morning raids by a state task force against the Gambino and Luchese crime families in Staten Island targeted their gambling, loan sharking and city contract bid-rigging operations.

"The biggest fish caught in the sweep was alleged Gambino capo Carmine Sciandra, who authorities say reaped the rewards from a multimillion-dollar sports-betting book while running the popular Top Tomato grocery chain."

Gotti Henchman Tony Roach Buggin' to
Get Out of Jail Early

(*Daily News*, New York, January 10, 2009)

"Anthony (Tony Roach) Rampino, a notorious hit man for late Gambino crime boss John Gotti, is getting a second shot at beating his 25-to-life sentence for heroin trafficking."

Politically Correct Mob Terms

Beating – anatomical rearrangement

Bid rigging – reducing economic uncertainty

Big gut – pasta storage facility

Car bomb – thermodynamic personnel decelerator

Chop shop – vocational education opportunity

Corpse in trunk – carpool lane compliant

Dead – actuarially mature

Drug trafficking – pharmaceutical relocation

Eats like a pig – reverse bulimia

Extortion – financial maintenance

Getaway car – emergency ground transportation

Hijacking a cargo truck – preemptive bargaining

Kill a politician – involuntary term limitation

Loan shark – purveyor of sub-prime stimulus package

Money laundering – recycling non-performing assets

Mug shot – pictorial identification

No-show job – vacation advance

Payoff – non-deductible investment

Protection money – cost-of-living adjustment

Skimming – tax-free distribution of revenue

Smash kneecaps – mobility inconvenienced

Six bullets through the chest – commitment to transparency

Stab – non-ballistic persuasion

Stool pigeon – associate who will soon be anatomically rearranged and carpool lane compliant

Torch a business – thermal warning

Torture – aggressive interrogation methods

Mob Words that Should Exist But Don't

badabingo – muscle in on old ladies gambling operation

breakhislego – order to destroy a kid's toy

icepicket – violent form of labor protest

prisonion – smell when paroled

RICOllect – to remember something after being threatened with a RICO prosecution

stabulate – count how many people you knifed this week

vignore – fail to pay interest to loan shark

whacknowledge – to admit you killed someone

wiretapestry – a fancy wall-hanging in which an electronic bug is hidden

Mobonics

Question: "What time is it?"
English answer: "Sorry, I don't know."
Mobonic answer: "Who wants ta know?"

Remark: "It's a beautiful day."
English response: "Sure is."
Mobonic response: "You gotta problem with that?"

Remark: "I hope things turn out OK."
English response: "Thanks."
Mobonic response: "Fuck you."

Remark: "Hurry up. Dinner's ready."
English response: "Be right there."
Mobonic response: "Fuck you."

Remark: "I like the tie you gave me. I wear it all the time."
English response: "Glad you like it."
Mobonic response: "Fuck you."

Mafia Shit List

While "Mafia" originally referred to an organized crime enterprise with roots in Italy, the word has evolved into a wider usage. Now it's often used to denote any group of experts who would force their standards on others. A perfect example is the "fashion Mafia." Members of this group can often be found commenting on celebrity apparel during award shows and other red carpet events. In fact, adding the word "Mafia" after any type of human endeavor produces a similar result. So we get the "cooking Mafia," the "movie Mafia," the "wine Mafia," etc.

This phenomenon also applies to the original meaning of "Mafia" as a criminal enterprise. By adding a nationality in front of the word, we get groups like the "Russian Mafia," the "Mexican Mafia," etc.

Here is the shit list for some of these Mafias.

Fashion Mafia – You look like shit.

Religion Mafia – Holy shit.

Bankruptcy Mafia – No shit.

Censorship Mafia – Cut the shit.

Charity Mafia – Who gives a shit?

Cooking Mafia – Eat shit.

Russian Mafia – Eat shit and die.

Mexican Mafia – Let's snort this shit.

Chinese Mafia – An hour later we'll give you more shit.

American Mafia – If shit happens, don't testify.

Headline Hits: Gotti and Bonanno

It's not just nick names that get the attention of punster headline writers. They can't resist playing off the real names of mobsters in the Gotti and Bonanno families. As always, these news scribes exhibit a keen sense of the obvious.

You Gotti Be Joking
(*The Sun*, London, November 29, 2007)

"WHO, me? Mafia mobster John Gotti Jr puts his hands up defensively as he denies being a police snitch."

Ahem, Judge, You Just Gotti Gimme Break
(*Daily News*, New York, July 3, 2008)

"Peter Gotti sounded more comedian than crime boss on Thursday as he bantered with a federal judge in an attempt to get a lighter sentence.

"The senior citizen gangster had hoped that a case of shrinking hemorrhoids and other health issues would shrink a 112-month sentence for racketeering and money laundering, but Judge Frederick Block said he looked just fine."

They've Gotti Bunch of Questions on Bail
(*Daily News*, New York, September 23, 1998)

"Reputed Mafia boss John A. (Junior) Gotti's efforts to get out of jail slowed to a crawl yesterday as prosecutors grilled his sister and brother-in-law about the $4 million mansion they've offered toward bail."

Capo's Gotti Gripes—
Says Boss Ko'd Plea Deal

(*New York Post*, May 24, 2004)

"A high-ranking Gambino mobster is boldly blaming reputed boss Peter Gotti for his legal woes, The Post has learned."

Yes, We Have No Bonannos

(*New York Post*, October 20, 2003)

"The Bonannos? Fuhggedaboutit. Now, they're the Massinos.

"One of the Big Apple's biggest crime families has changed its name, revealed mob expert Kenneth McCabe...."

Peeled Bonannos—Godfathers Among 27
Nailed in Fed Bust

(*New York Post*, January 21, 2004)

"The feds hit a Bonanno bonanza yesterday, rounding up more than two dozen reputed wiseguys in a crushing blow to the crime family."

Feds Pick Bunch of Bonannos

(*New York Post*, October 8, 2009)

"The troubled Bonanno crime family took another crippling blow from the feds yesterday as 15 reputed mobsters were hit with a sweeping racketeering indictment—based partly on the grand-jury testimony of boss-turned-stoolie Joseph Massino."

Yes, They Have One Bonanno

(Daily News, New York, March 19, 2004)

"And then there was one.

"Bonanno boss Joseph Massino will be the lone defendant at his murder trial next month after Brooklyn prosecutors notched their 28th guilty plea in a federal racketeering case.

"'We're definitely going to trial,' said Massino's lawyer, David Breitbart. 'It's going to be a war.'"

Mob Haikus

Judge banging gavel
Rats squeal and canaries sing
Sleep with fish

Make offer
Refusal flutters in wind
Blood splashes

Wise guys in restaurant
Gunfire eats my screams
Smoke shaped like pasta

Stoolie sculpture
Ice pick chases eyes
Cement shoes play in puddle

Weather report
Blue corpse and cold
Hail of bullets

Car bomb explodes
Beautiful, strange blossoms fall
Burned hatred dances

CHAPTER TWELVE
More Headline Hits

As discussed previously, many newspapers delight in reporting news about organized crime with stories that include puns in their headlines. In this chapter we'll examine specific mob-related terms that often prove irresistible for headline writers around the world.

The first is "godfather." Like the title of the famous movie, godfather refers to the top boss of an organized crime group. So when a godfather is involved in a potential story, it's automatically news. It's also likely that the word "godfather" will be used in the headline as he will be the most newsworthy figure. And that means headline writers can have a blast coming up with variations of the term.

Here are a few.

Gotchafather

(*The Sun*, London, November 6, 2007)

"THE Mafia's top Godfather was captured yesterday when 40 armed cops stormed his hideaway.

"Salvatore Lo Piccolo—held with his son Sandro and two other Mob bosses—had been on the run for NINETEEN years."

Why The Gayfather Had to Be Whacked; Hit man Killed Homosexual Mafia Boss Out of 'Shame'

(*The Mirror*, London, May 2, 2003)

"A hit man stunned a packed courtroom yesterday by claiming he gunned down a Mafia godfather because he was gay.

"Gangster Anthony Capo said he feared the DeCavalcante crime family would become the laughing stock of the underworld if their acting Don, John 'Johnny Boy' D'Amato, was ever outed."

The Blobfather

(*The Sun*, London, March 13, 2008)

"Porky Salvatore Ferranti, 36, was put under house arrest accused of being a Mafia mobster—as his 33st frame is too big for jails in Sicily."

The God-Fatter

(*The Daily Mail*, London, November 8, 2008)

"A mobster was nicked in hospital as he awoke from liposuction surgery—by cops dressed as nurses in Cosenza, Italy."

Gone-Father Gotti Makes a Don Deal

(*Daily News*, New York, November 24th 1996)

"John Gotti, the swaggering crime chieftain now in prison for life, has agreed to turn over the reins of the powerful Gambino crime family to a Brooklyn underling, sources have told the *Daily News*.

"Under pressure from the Commission, the Mafia's ruling panel of New York crime families, Gotti will relinquish his post as leader of the 200-member Gambino family to 56-year-old Nicholas (Little Nick) Corozzo, a Brooklyn-based capo."

Tough Nut Cracks—'Oddfather' Fesses Up to 30-Yr. Act

(*New York Post*, April 8, 2003)

"Vincent 'Chin' Gigante has admitted he's crazy like a fox.

"In a bizarre end to a legendary 30-year saga, the Genovese boss boldly dropped his 'Oddfather' act yesterday—showing that his mumbling, stumbling ways were all part of an elaborate ruse designed to foil the feds.

"Alert, animated and moving under his own steam, Gigante, 75, walked into court to plead guilty to obstructing justice.

"There he flashed frequent grins and chatted with his son, Andrew Gigante.

"It was a dramatic transformation for the mobster best known for his habit of wandering around Greenwich Village in an old bathrobe and slippers."

Another mob-related term beloved of punning headline writers is "wiseguy." It refers to a person who has been officially inducted into the Mafia. And most important, it's easy to rhyme with other words. For example:

The 'Rise' Guys—W'chester Docs Charged with Giving Mob Viagra

(*New York Post*, May 6, 2005)

"Three Westchester doctors were busted yesterday for providing Gambino mobsters large quantities of Viagra and other sex pills in exchange for favors—like coveted seating at the legendary eatery Rao's, the feds charged yesterday."

The Cries-Guy
G-Man's Lawyer Busts Sobster's Bawls
(*New York Post*, October 23, 2007)

"This sob-fella is a repeat offender.

"Under cross-examination yesterday in the trial of accused rogue FBI Agent Lindley DeVecchio, Mafia hit man Larry Mazza conceded that his tearful breakdown on the stand last Thursday wasn't his first.

"'Isn't it a fact that it's the same point where you began to cry in the grand jury?' lawyer Douglas Grover asked, referring to the one-time Colombo soldier's waterworks while discussing his fall into a life of crime after studying to be a cop or firefighter."

Bonanno 'Lies Guy' Now Risks Lethal Jab
(*Daily News*, New York, April 3rd 2007)

"A dopey Mafia don thought a lie-detector test might save his life. He didn't figure he'd flunk.

"Now, former acting Bonanno crime family boss Vincent (Vinny Gorgeous) Basciano is facing the death penalty for allegedly ordering a gangland murder."

Mob G-Man Became One of Wide Guys.
'I Gained A Good 80 Pounds'
(*Daily News*, New York, May 17, 2006)

"THE MAN WHO infiltrated the mob gained more than 80 pounds in his first two years—learning that the GoodFellas were more like FatFellas, eating their way through New York."

The third mob-related term that excites headline writers is "goodfellas." Like the term godfather, it was also the title of a popular movie. It refers to members of the Mafia. Here are a few examples.

Is Gumfella Telling Whole Tooth?
(*Daily News*, New York, June 10, 2005)

"THE MAFIA MAY BE losing its bite.

"Jailed reputed mob boss Dominick (Quiet Dom) Cirillo is making some noise behind bars, claiming he needs new choppers so he can get back to eating solid prison food.

"Cirillo, 75, says he has been reduced to slurping oatmeal and grits bought at the Metropolitan Detention Center commissary because his back teeth were recently removed.

"The wiseguy's lawyer is trying to get the reputed head of the Genovese crime family, who is awaiting trial on racketeering charges, out on a furlough to get dentures from his personal dentist so that he can chew again."

Lostfella Still Makes Impact on Mob Trial
(*Daily News*, New York, October 18, 2005)

"HIS CHAIR AT the defense table remains empty, but missing wiseguy Lawrence Ricci is hardly forgotten at the waterfront corruption trial in federal court.

"A pair of mob rats testified yesterday that Ricci was a key player in the Genovese crime family's branch in New Jersey."

Oldfella Felled After Plea Snub

(*New York Post*, March 16, 2004)

"A geriatric mobster facing double-murder charges suffered chest pains in court yesterday and was rushed to the hospital after a federal judge rejected a plea deal as his trial was set to begin."

Let Me Be Pretty Fella,
Mob Guy Asks Judge

(*Daily News*, New York, February 8 2007)

"HE MIGHT have done bad, but he still needs to look good.

"A reputed Queens gangster, stuck inside under house arrest, told a federal judge he needs to duck out for six hours a month—to get a pedicure and a haircut."

Ghostfella's Li'l Chop of Horrors
Wiseguy Bares Slay at SI 'Haunted' House
(*New York Post*, October 15, 20008)

"In this haunted house, prosecutors didn't need the walls to talk.

"A mob turncoat testified in grisly detail yesterday how a member of his crew brutally hacked and drowned a man at a spooky Staten Island mansion, then had his body sawed up and burned the pieces in a furnace."

Fakefella Undercover at Trial
(*Daily News*, New York, May 3, 2006)

"FEDERAL PROSECUTORS want to close a Manhattan courtroom for the testimony of an undercover FBI agent who played the role of mobster 'Jack Falcone' so well that wiseguys wanted to induct him into the Mafia."

A Wed-Fella
Gotti Capo Freed to Get Nup License
(*New York Post*, December 6, 2007)

"One way or another, his life as a free man is nearly over.

"Reputed Gambino capo George DeCicco, 78, and his longtime girlfriend, Gail Lombardozzi, 52, yesterday got a marriage license—a year after feds indicted the high-powered capo, who had successfully ducked prosecution for decades.

"A federal judge allowed the gray-haired mobster—who is under house arrest pending his racketeering and loan-sharking trial—to leave his home for a few hours yesterday so he and Lombardozzi could take a ride over to Staten Island Borough Hall to get the license."

Victim A 'Gun Fella'
—Stabber: I Feared for Life

(*New York Post*, August 4, 2004)

"A reputed Genovese soldier, accused of murdering his brother-in-law, claims it was self-defense because the victim not only beat him with a stickball bat—but also threatened to shoot him.

"Andrew Garguilo—whom the feds once considered the biggest bookmaker on the East Coast—maintains he had no choice but to stab 57-year-old Preston Geritano to death inside Amici restaurant in Bay Ridge last spring."

'Studfellas' Father Families from Prison

(*The Telegraph*, London, England, March 2002)

"The wife of a jailed mobster is so determined to keep the 'Mafia family' going that she is suing the United States Justice Department for the return of a vial of her husband's frozen sperm.

"The case is the latest twist in the 'Studfella' scandal in which jailed Mafia members from New York and New Jersey have been caught bribing guards to smuggle their semen to wives and 'goumadas,' or mistresses."

Sounds Like a Scared-Fella

(*New York Post*, November 23, 2009)

"Ever hear of the mob enforcer who's afraid of trick-or-treating kids? Charles 'Fat Charlie' Salzano, a 370-pound leg-breaker for the Genovese gang, already did 32 months behind bars for threatening to cripple a couple of businessmen who were late with their loan-shark payments, Jerry Capeci reports on his GangLand Web site. Released in August, Salzano's now confined to his home as he awaits trial for racketeering. But last month, the tough guy was granted permission by Manhattan federal Judge Richard Holwell to spend Halloween at his brother's house. His lawyer argued that Salzano, 59, has a heart problem and his wife was going to be out. 'As a result, he'd be home alone at their Valley Stream condo, forced to face dozens of neighborhood kids in scary costumes ringing the bell and screaming for treats—all by himself,' Capeci wrote. 'Prosecutors did not object (maybe they were laughing too hard).'"

Good (Bye) Fellas
Feds: Massive Indictment Shatters Dying Mob Empire

(*Boston Herald*, April 9. 1997)

"A blockbuster federal murder and racketeering indictment unsealed yesterday portrays a 1990s Boston Mob as divided and cannibalistic—with wiseguys and wannabes fighting and killing over the still-profitable scraps of a dying empire."

CHAPTER THIRTEEN
Not So Wise Guys

On March 13, 1998, the *Daily News* ran an article about "what could be the city's dumbest mobster." Here's the story. On February 4, 1994, a college student was stabbed to death outside a mob bar. Eight hours later, just before noon, an FBI agent was parked by a fast food restaurant in the area. He observed a man drive up in a Mercedes, exit the car, look around nervously and throw two paper bags into a Dumpster. The FBI agent recognized the man as Luchese crime family capo Anthony "Blue Eyes" Santorelli. When the mobster left, the agent checked the Dumpster and found bloody clothes. A DNA check showed the clothes belonged to the murdered college student.

The article quoted an unnamed witness who testified in the case. Here's what he had to say:

> Blue Eyes has to be the world's dumbest wise guy. He drives in that neighborhood at high noon and doesn't see an FBI agent in the car? The FBI guy isn't even undercover. In that neighborhood, they are probably the only two white guys around. And my boss doesn't make the agent's car? Ridiculous. Blue Eyes brought down his whole gang with this idiocy.

By the way, the article was headlined: "A Case of Dumb And Dumpster."

So what can we learn from this story? Three things. First, staying away from fast food places really *is* good for your health—and freedom. Second, if you're gonna throw a murder victim's clothes in a public Dumpster, wash the blood out of them first. And third, wise guys aren't always wise.

In this chapter, you'll find more examples and jokes about what the media likes to refer to as "Dumbfellas."

Leave the gun; take the cannoli.

Top 6 Signs You're Dealing with a Dumb Mobster

Gives you a pinky ring for your birthday—it still has the pinky.

Thinks skim milk is a mob operation.

Can't blend into witness protection on Halloween.

Doesn't take the Fifth because he can't count that high.

Tries to dig his way out of a grave.

Uses a baseball bat to play baseball.

Highjack High Jinx

While driving along the back roads of a small town, two mobsters who hijacked a truck came to an overpass with a sign that read "CLEARANCE 11'3."

They got out and measured their rig, which was 12'4.

"What do you think?" one asked the other.

The driver looked around carefully, then shifted into first. "Not a cop in sight. Let's take a chance!"

Getaway Car

Did you hear about the mobster who tried to make a new kind of getaway car?

No.

He took the engine from a Ford, the transmission from an Oldsmobile, the tires from a Cadillac, and the exhaust system from a Plymouth.

Really? What did he get?

Fifteen years for auto theft.

Career Planning

A detective was going through a mobster's rap sheet. "This is quite a record you have," the detective said. "Loan sharking, drug running, armed robbery, kidnapping, burglary, auto theft, shoplifting, money laundering."

"I know," replied the mobster. "It took me quite some time to figure out what I was good at."

Follow Instructions

Vinny and Sal are taking care of some business out at the docks. Suddenly Sal grabs his chest and falls to the ground. He doesn't seem to be breathing and his eyes are rolled back in his head. Vinny whips out his cell phone and calls 911. He gasps to the operator, "I think Sal is dead! What should I do?"

The operator, in a calm soothing voice says, "Just take it easy and follow my instructions. First, let's make sure he's dead."

There is a silence. Then a shot is heard.

Vinny's voice comes back on the line, "OK... now what?"

Lie Detector

A mob godfather, a mob capo, and a mob soldier take a lie detector test.

The godfather says: "I think I can drink 10 bottles of wine".

BUZZZZZZ, goes the lie detector.

"OK," he says, "5 bottles".

And the machine is silent.

The capo says: "I think I can eat 10 plates of pasta".

BUZZZZZZ, goes the lie detector.

"All right, 5 plates".

And the machine is silent.

The soldier says: "I think..."

BUZZZZZZ goes the machine.

More Dumbfella Stuff

Q: Why was the stupid hit man hospitalized?
A: He was sent to blow up a car and burned his lips on the tailpipe.

Q: What do a mob soldier and a fifteen-watt light bulb have in common?
A: Neither one is very bright.

Q: What's the difference between a community organizer and a dumb hit man?
A: There aren't any movies about community organizers.

Judge: "I thought I told you I never wanted to see you in here again."
Mobster: "That's what I told the cops, but they wouldn't listen."

Headline Hits: Dumbfellas

Murder Trial for Mafia 'Dumbfella'
(*The Times*, London, July 24, 2004)

"The son of the New York Mafia chieftain John Gotti has been charged with ordering a botched 1992 hit on an anti-crime crusader who dared to call his father 'Public Enemy No 1'. John Gotti Jr., whose late father was the head of the Gambino crime family, is accused of trying to kill Curtis Sliwa, the founder of the Guardian Angels vigilante group that patrolled New York in red berets during the crime wave of the 1980s."

'Dumbfella' Boasts of Cop-Kill on Tape
(*New York Post*, May 17, 2001)

"An accused cop killer gleefully boasted his cold-blooded slaying of an off-duty officer was proof-positive he could be trusted as a Mafia hit man, tapes played in a Queens court revealed yesterday."

No Hits, 1 Error –
Dumbfella Targeted 2 Feds by Mistake
(*New York Post*, May 20, 2003)

"Mob turncoat Vincent 'Vinny Ocean' Palermo testified yesterday how he was within seconds of killing two FBI agents who Mafia bosses believed were hit men—but the 'family' *consigliere* saved him from making the fatal mistake."

Don't Do The Crime If You Can't Do The PUN-ishment

The New Job

This guy, Artie, gets tired of working so hard and not getting anywhere, and seeing all these guys in the Mafia in their fine three-piece suits and fancy cars, decides that he has to join the Mafia. He goes up to one of the guys and says, " I want to join the Mafia."

The guy answers, "You ever kill anyone for money?"

Artie answers, "No."

The guy says, " Well, you either got to be born into the Mafia, or you gotta kill somebody for money."

So Artie says, " How much will you pay me?"

The guy says, " I'm not gonna pay you."

Artie says, " C'mon, just pay me a dollar so I can get in."

The guy says, "OK, I'll tell you what. You kill somebody, tell me about it, and if I see it in the morning paper, I'll pay you a dollar."

Artie says, " Oh thank you, thank you!" and heads off on his mission. He goes to Ralph's Supermarket, sees an old lady pushing a cart, and decides that she's lived a full life, goes up to her, grabs her around the neck and chokes her to death.

The bag boy sees him and chases after him. Artie realizes that he can't outrun the bag boy, turns around, grabs the bag boy by the neck, and chokes him to death.

In the morning paper the headlines read, "ARTIE CHOKES TWO FOR A DOLLAR AT RALPH'S!"

The Eccentric Hit Man

Big Louie the Torpedo was becoming increasingly curious about one of the newer members of his mob, Benny the Rod. Benny had been in the business for many years in another part of the country. During that time he had garnered quite a reputation for being the most conscientious and honorable hit man available. He was also considered quite eccentric, perhaps odd, in that for the last ten years or so he always kept one hand in his pocket—clutching his cold steel weapon in readiness (hence the nickname, Benny the Rod). When Benny arrived at Louie's office, the question was put to him. "So what's the story with you and this here gun of yours, eh? Like, are you scared or somethin' or you just want to always be ready or what?"

"Not scared ..." Benny growled, "been doin' it dis way ever since me sister-in-law's weddin' 'bout ten years ago now."

"Oh yeah? ... so ...?"

"Well, I used ta know her fiancé at da time—a no-good chiseler. He never even loved the goil so much ... but he made her happy and so I kept me mouth shut about it," Benny explained.

Louie leaned in, expecting the point of the matter. "And since dat time I gotta do it dis way."

"But WHY?!" Louie finally demanded?

"Well, I was at da wedding," grumbled Benny, "and I wasn't about to say nuttin' about it then, so now I gotta do like da preacher said, 'Speak Now or Forever Hold Your Piece!'"

Flower Business

The Mafia in a city in Italy had a monopoly on the flower business. They overcharged for everything. And many people couldn't afford flowers for weddings or funerals. Two Catholic priests decided to do something about it. They started a flower business with low prices that everyone could afford. Soon everyone shopped there instead of buying the overpriced flowers from the Mafia. This worried the Mafia godfathers because the flowers were their only legitimate income. They held a meeting to plan a response. Finally, they decided to send Hue, their biggest and meanest soldier, after the priests. Hue went to the priests, made some threats and shut their business down. And the Mafia flower monopoly was restored. What's the moral of this story? Hue, and only Hue, can stop Florist Friars!

You Can't Make This Stuff Up

Till Debt Do Us Part

On January 25, 1998, *The New York Times* reported the death of Gambino crime family associate Joseph Conigliaro. Mr. Conigliaro had become a legendary "dumbfella" 25 years earlier. On November 1, 1973, Conigliaro and another mobster, James Gallo, were supposed to collect a debt from Vincent Ensulo aka Vinnie Ba Ba. After spotting Ensulo in Brooklyn, Conigliaro and Gallo forced their way into his car. Ensulo was seated between them. And they each had a gun pointed at him.

After travelling a few blocks, Ensulo grabbed the steering wheel. Conigliaro and Gallo opened fire. But the car swerved and they shot each other. Conigliaro was confined to a wheel chair for the rest of his life. According to the *Daily News*, every year since then Vinny Ensulo sent wheelchair batteries to Conigliaro. They were always accompanied by a card that read, "Keep rolling, from your best pal, Vinny Ba Ba."

Mob Full Deckisms

All brass and no knuckles.

A little light in the envelope.

Not the sharpest ice pick in the drawer.

Not enough chalk on the pool cue.

A few pulls short of a jackpot.

The lights are on but nobody's on parole.

A few tables short of a casino.

House arrest bracelet is missing a few batteries.

If brains were gasoline, he couldn't torch a dollhouse.

Two dice short of a craps game.

His brain took the Fifth.

A mind as sharp as a mug shot.

Couldn't pick himself out of a lineup.

His pool table is missing a few balls.

A 12 gauge IQ in a semi-automatic world.

A few badda bings short of a boom.

About the Author

Malcolm Kushner, "America's Favorite Humor Consultant," is an internationally acclaimed expert on humor and communication. He is the author of *The Light Touch: How to Use Humor for Business Success, Public Speaking For Dummies, Vintage Humor For Wine Lovers* and *California Squisine: Healthy Food That's Fast Fun And Squeezable For Kids*. He is also the cocreator of a humor exhibit that appeared at the Ronald Reagan Presidential Library.

Kushner has been profiled in *Time Magazine, USA Today, The New York Times* and *The Washington Post*. His television and radio appearances include CNN, C-SPAN, Fox & Friends, National Public Radio, CNBC, "Voice of America" and "The Larry King Show." *The Wall Street Journal* has called him "irrepressible."

A popular speaker at corporate and association meetings, Kushner has keynoted everywhere from The Smithsonian Institution to the Inc. 500 Conference. He is based in Menasha, Wisconsin.

Visit his websites at
www.kushnergroup.com
www.museumofhumor.com

He can be reached at
mk@kushnergroup.com

Malcolm Kushner & Associates
P.O. Box 668
Menasha, WI 54952

Robert D. Reed Publishers Order Form

Call in your order for fast service and quantity discounts
(541) 347- 9882

OR order on-line at **www.rdrpublishers.com** *using PayPal.*
OR order by mail:
Make a copy of this form; enclose payment information:
Robert D. Reed Publishers
1380 Face Rock Drive, Bandon, OR 97411
Fax at (541) 347-9883

Send indicated books to:

Name_____

Address _____

City _____ State _____ Zip _____

Phone _____ Fax _____ Cell _____

E-Mail_____

Payment by check ☐ or credit card ☐ *(All major credit cards are accepted.)*

Name on card _____

Card Number _____

Exp. Date _____ Last 3-Digit number on back of card_____

Qty.

The Official Book of Mob Humor by Malcolm Kushner .... $9.95 _____

HOUSECALLS: How we all can heal the world
one visit at a time by Patch Adams .... $11.95 _____

Shooting the Mailbox by Curkendall, Richards, & Hatton .... $14.95 _____

Two Guys Read the Obituaries
by Steve Chandler and Terrence Hill .... $14.95 _____

Hobo Sapien: Freight Train Hopping Tao and Zen
by Wayne Iverson.. $12.95 _____

Die Laughing: Lighthearted Views of a
Grave Situation by Steve Mickle .... $11.95 _____

Math Jokes 4 Mathy Folks by Patrick Vennebush .... $11.95 _____

Total Number of Books _____ Total Amount _____

Note: Shipping is $3.50 1st book + $1 for each additional book.   Shipping _____

THE TOTAL_____

192